SAINT T

SAINT THOMAS AQUINAS

Teacher of Truth

Francis John Selman

Francis J. Selman

T&T CLARK
EDINBURGH

T&T CLARK LTD
59 GEORGE STREET
EDINBURGH EH2 2LQ
SCOTLAND

Nihil obstat: Aidan Nichols O.P. M.A. S.T.L. Censor
Imprimatur: +   Alan C. Clark
Bishop of East Anglia
Poringland 6 October 1992

The Nihil obstat and Imprimatur are a declaration that a book is considered to
be free from doctrinal or moral error. It is not implied that those who have
granted the Nihil obstat and Imprimatur agree with the contents, opinions or
statements expressed.

First published 1994

ISBN 0 567 29245 2

British Library Cataloguing in Publication Data
A catalogue record for this book is available
from the British Library

Typeset by Trinity Typesetting, Edinburgh
Printed and bound in Great Britain by Redwood Books, Wiltshire

*To my Mother
and in memory
of my Father*

Contents

Preface

The writings of St Thomas Aquinas are like an inexhaustible fount; this book is drawn from only a small part of all that he wrote. It is intended for those who would like to know quite briefly what he says about the principal parts of the Christian faith. Thus I use as much as possible within its short compass the words of St Thomas himself. Since one cannot have the theology of St Thomas without the philosophy, for they go together in him in his elucidation of the Faith, I include an account of his philosophy, which retains its interest for today. However, it may be better not to decide how much St Thomas is philosopher or theologian but simply to see him as he set out to be in whatever matter he was inquiring about: a teacher of truth.

I am grateful to Aidan Nichols O.P. for his suggestions and for pointing out some errors. The quotation from *Troilus and Cressida* in chapter 5 I owe to the late Kenelm Foster O.P., who also drew my attention to the first seven or so chapters of St Thomas' *Summa contra Gentiles*, Book I, which he often reread. Perhaps it was reading *God and the Soul* by Peter Geach, which first led me to read St Thomas himself.

F. J. Selman
Cambridge
September 1992

Since men are ordered by divine providence to a higher good than human frailty can experience in the present life, the mind has to be called up to something higher than our reason can attain presently, so that it may learn to desire and study to aim at something which altogether surpasses the state of our present life.

Contra Gentiles I c. 5.

1

Introduction

The course of St Thomas' life was influenced by two events of the early thirteenth century: the rise of the new universities in Europe and the introduction of new thought from Aristotle into them. The university of Paris received its statutes from Pope Innocent III in 1215. For a long time Aristotle had only been known in the West for his works on logic until the bulk of his writings was first brought to the West by the Arabic scholars who came to Spain. To see St Thomas in historical perspective, he stands a little closer to us in time than he did to St Augustine, who died in 430 and had been the dominant influence on thought in the West up to the time of St Thomas.

St Thomas came from a noble family since his father, Landulf, was descended from the counts of Aquino. Thomas was born in 1225 or 1226 and, at the age of five, sent to school at Montecassino. But when the neighbourhood became troubled, he moved from there to Naples, where he made his first acquaintance with the thought of Aristotle at university. In Naples he joined, in 1242, the Dominican Order of Preachers, which had been approved by Honorius III in 1216. Two years later he was sent to Paris but was captured on the way by his brothers, since his family was opposed to his decision to enter a mendicant order. Their own hope had been that he would one day increase the family estates by becoming the abbot of Montecassino. St Thomas used the year of his imprisonment for acquiring his extensive knowledge of Scripture, which was perhaps nearly all that he had then to read.

When he did reach Paris, in 1246, he found St Albert the Great, who was already making extensive use of Aristotle,

1

lecturing there. In 1248 they went together to Cologne, where Thomas studied under Albert for the next four years. It was in Cologne that Thomas heard Albert's lectures on Pseudo-Dionysius, whom St Thomas quotes about as much as he does St Augustine. This author wrote in the early sixth century, possibly in Syria. In 1252 St Thomas returned with St Albert to Paris, where he took up teaching for the next seven years. In Paris he wrote his commentary on the *Sentences* of Peter Lombard, 1254-1256, and from 1256-1259 his first major set of disputed questions, *De Veritate*, named after the topic of the first question — on truth. When St Thomas became a Master himself, in 1256, he took as the text for his inaugural lecture, 'watering the mountains from things above' (*Psalm* 104, 13), which he applies to teachers, who are like mountains receiving wisdom from above. Before he left Paris, in 1259, he had begun the *Summa contra Gentiles*, which may have been intended as a handbook for preachers to use when addressing Moors in Spain. In this work he lays out reasons for the Christian faith, since he says that in arguing with those who do not accept the same Scriptures appeal has to be made to reason, to which all alike are compelled to assent. It was completed in Orvieto in 1264.

St Thomas returned to Naples in 1260 and from 1261-64 was in Orvieto, where Urban IV had his papal court. He spent the second half of his Italian period, 1265-68, in Rome setting up a house of studies for his Order there. In Rome he wrote his questions *De Potentia*, 1265-66, and *De Malo*, 1266-67, and his own commentary on the *Divine Names* of Pseudo-Dionysius. In 1266 he began his masterpiece, the *Summa theologiae*, which he states in the prologue is intended 'for little ones', and with which he was occupied for almost the rest of his life, between writing other great works, until a few months before he died he had a vision which made all he had written seem 'like straw'.

He then returned for a third spell in Paris, 1269-72, when he was engaged in controversy with the Averroists, who called forth from his pen the treatise *De Unitate Intellectus* (1270), and possibly the *Quaestiones de Anima* (1269-70), to be distinguished from his commentary on the *De Anima* of Aristotle. In the course of his life St Thomas lectured on almost the entire works of Aristotle. His massive commentary on the *Metaphysics* belongs to this third time in Paris, being written from 1270-72. He also wrote several commentaries on books of Scripture: on *Job, Isaiah,* the Gospels of *St Matthew* and *St John* (only the first five chapters of this by Thomas himself, the rest from lecture notes made by his secretary, Reginald of Piperno), and all the *Epistles of St Paul,* which were probably written in Naples 1272-73. He says that the theme of *Job,* for instance, is that human affairs are ruled by divine providence and we are not to expect that good and evil will be appropriately repaid in this life since retribution does not come in this life alone. St Thomas died on the 7 March 1274, shortly after setting out from Naples for the Council of Lyon. He was canonized by John XXII in 1323.

Perhaps, if one had asked St Thomas what he was doing in writing on theology, he would have replied that he was drawing out the meaning of Scripture, in which he says things are found hidden and dispersed.[1] In the Middle Ages the highest honour for a teacher in the faculty of theology was to be permitted to lecture on Scripture on one's own. St Thomas' works may be compared with the Preludes and Fugues of Bach in their continuous working out of themes on basic principles. The other name of this work of music, *Das wohl temperierte Klavier* (The well-tempered harpsicord) seems an apt description of the temper of St Thomas' own writings, which display his calm, dispassionate but trenchant mind. If St Thomas' writings seem long to us, they are so because it is only by setting out clearly all the strands in the existence of things that we can then begin to gain some view of them in their simple outlines, just as an artist who can depict an object with a few simple lines has first seen it quite accurately. St Thomas notes that we have no simple apprehension of the truth in this life but we have to search into it with reasoning.

For St Thomas theology is properly wisdom. He still held the ancient conception of wisdom, that the wise man is the good ruler since he knows how to order and direct things. Since things get their order from the end they are for, the wise person will consider the end of things, and this will lead to considering

[1] *Summa* II-II 1, 9.

the end of all things, of the universe. As things get their end from their maker, considering the end, or purpose, of the universe will also involve considering its source. Wisdom differs from mere science since, as we see today, it requires wisdom to use our scientific knowledge well for our good. A pharmacist, for example, may be able to tell you all about the properties of the medicines he makes but a physician requires wisdom in knowing which to use in each case for his end, which is to heal his patients.

The end of the whole universe, St Thomas says, is truth, since things get their end from their maker and the maker of the universe is a Mind. The good of the mind is truth. The wisdom which inquires about the end of all things does not just consider this or that area of truth, as the various sciences do, but that truth which is the source of all truth.[2] There are two ways of knowing truth: many things are accessible to natural reason but there are some things which we only know about God by faith in what has been revealed about them. However, faith and reason are not in opposition to one another since the author of revelation and of our reason is the same; whatever is contrary to right reason is also contrary to divine wisdom. The use of reason in explaining belief is to show that faith is not impossible or contradictory to reason. St Thomas has no place for the double truth theory, which was later espoused by William of Ockham (1287-1347), according to which valid reasoning may be passed over in matters of faith. For St Thomas there are not two standards of truth but two ways of knowing truth. He would not have approved of a view common in this century, that there are different kinds of truth: logical truth, scientific truth, historical truth, religious truth and so on. For truth is one.

St Thomas defines truth as the correspondence (*adequatio*) of the mind with the thing (*res*, from which we get our word 'reality'). Truth is a correspondence since Thomas decides that truth is first of all in that in which its opposite, falsehood, is found. This is in the mind rather than in things. A thought is true when there is something in reality to which it corresponds.

[2]*Contra Gentiles* I c. 1.

Truth goes together with existence in St Thomas since truth concerns knowledge and things can only be known as they are existent. Truth and being are interchangeable, he says, because things are only knowable as they exist. The first thing that comes into our mind about something is that it exists; whatever else we may know about it: its size, shape, colour, etc., we first apprehend it as something existent. Our minds are not true because things are true but because they *exist*.[3] Truth is founded on the existent, he says.[4] The truth in our minds comes from the existence of things but the truth of God's mind does not come from the existence of things since they get their existence from him. One thing could not be true by another unless we come back to something existent which is not true by another but is its own truth. Not only is there truth in God's mind but he is Truth. God is the First Truth since he is the source of all existence; he is 'the fountain and source of the whole of existence and truth', *fons et principium totius esse et veritatis*.[5] Thus there is one Truth by which all things are true as they are existent because of him.

However abstract Aquinas may seem to modern readers, he is an existentialist in the true sense of the word since he is as interested in the existence of real things as any philosopher has ever been. He is more truly an existentialist than modern existentialists, who mainly consider the transitory conditions of human existence, since he is concerned with all existence. We have only to compare the few times that '*esse*', the word in him for existence, occurs in a small early work of his, *De Ente et Essentia* (On Being and Essence), which he wrote around 1252, with its much more frequent use in his later *Summa*, to appreciate how the notion of existence came to assume an increasingly key role in his thought.

[3]*Summa* I 16, 1 ad 3.
[4]*Ibid.* I 16, 3 ad 2.
[5]*Ibid.* I 12, 8 ad 4.

2

God

For St Thomas theology is, as the word suggests, foremost about God; it is discourse about God (*sermo de deo*). In what we can know and say about God he distinguishes between what we can know by using the light of reason and what we would never know about God unless it had been revealed to us. By natural reason we can know *that* God exists but he is insistent that we cannot know *what* God is. What St Thomas says on this point was grasped well by Hobbes: 'the nature of God is incomprehensible; that is to say, we understand nothing of what he is, but only *that he is*'.[1] We do not know what God is because the divine light is hidden from us on account of its simplicity.[2] 'We are joined to God as to the unknown', St Thomas says, quoting from Pseudo-Dionysius.[3] However, this does not mean that we cannot know anything at all about God, since he goes on to say in the very next sentence that we know him more fully as we attribute to him some things from revelation, which natural reason cannot arrive at, such as that he is three and one. If God were utterly unknown to us, St Paul would not have said to the Athenians on the Areopagus that he could tell them who was the unknown God to whom they had dedicated an altar — the God who created the world (*Acts* 17, 23). Nor would St Thomas himself have said that his intention in writing theology was to convey a knowledge of God, '*cognitionem dei tradere*'. He also says that we can reach up to, or

---

[1] *Leviathan* Pt III c. 34.
[2] *De Divinis Nominibus* IV lect. 1.
[3] *Summa* I 12, 13 ad 1.

touch (*attingere*), God by knowing and loving him. Because God is altogether above everything, it does not follow that he cannot be known in any way at all but that he surpasses anything we can know about him, which means that we do not *comprehend* him.[4] Perhaps St Thomas' last word on what we can know about God is that it is more apparent to us what God is *not* than what he is.[5] We know God more the more we understand that he exceeds everything we can understand about him.[6] However, not being able to say what God is does not mean that we cannot use the word 'God' since we can accept what God stands for, someone who exists above everything else, by demonstrating his existence from effects as their cause.[7] Not being able to define words does not prevent us from using them properly: try to define fire, for instance, using simple words.

For St Thomas the way that we can know that God exists is as the cause of effects. To show that God exists, we have to begin, he says, with the things we see and do know. This is not so different from a method used by natural scientists, of supposing that some observed effect is due to an unseen cause, for example Bequerel's 'invisible rays'. Becquerel noticed that uranium which had not been previously exposed to sunlight induced phosphorescence on photographic plates kept in the dark and concluded that this was due to rays emanating from the uranium itself. These rays were later distinguished as alpha, beta and gamma rays. Modern physicists themselves have declared that there is no known source of inertia in the world. St Thomas presents a set of five arguments, known as 'the Five ways', which can be found in Aristotle, for showing that God exists. It is worth going through these arguments since other things which Thomas says about God can then be seen to derive from them.

St Thomas' first way of showing that God exists is to start with something about which he says everyone agrees: that there is

[4]*Ibid.* I 12, 1 ad 3.
[5]*Ibid.* I 1, 9 ad 3.
[6]*Ibid.* II-II 8, 7.
[7]*Ibid.* I 2, 2 ad 2.

motion in the world. Since nothing moves of itself unless it is moved, if one thing is moved by another we must come back to something which moves without being moved. Movement for St Thomas is the change of something, since this can be regarded as the transition to something which it can be: a caterpillar which is a potential butterfly changes into an actual butterfly. Since something actual must precede what is potential, God always is all that he is. It would be inappropriate to say 'or can be', for there is nothing which God could become which he is not already, since this would imply that he is mutable and imperfect. If God were not immutable this would take away his simplicity.

St Thomas' second way is that there is a series of one thing causing another, but if every cause itself needed a cause there would not be any chain of cause and effect at all. Since one thing is the cause of another, there must be a first cause. But if we go back in an infinite regression, we would never come to a first cause. So we come back to a cause which has no cause. However, this should not make us think or say that God is the cause of himself; there is nothing caused in God.

The third way is that we would not have a world of contingent things, that is of things which might or might not happen to be, unless there were some necessary being. Thomas' word for contingent is 'possibles' since they are things which can exist and not exist by coming into and going out of existence. If everything were like this there would not be anything, since what can be at one time was not; so there would be nothing because what is not can only come into existence through something which already exists. So for contingent things to exist there must be some necessary thing. Necessary things either get their necessity from something else or they are necessary through themselves. Thus things which are necessary through something else bring us back to something existent which is necessary of itself.

The fourth way argues that we could not talk of things being more or less, such as more or less just, unless there were something which is most that thing and with which all other things are compared. We measure things as more or less just by justice itself. Likewise, for things to be more or less true there is something which is most true. We might say that the more something is real, that is true, gold the more it simply *is* gold. Aristotle argues that what is most true is also most being since it does not come to be or cease to be true. Thus he concludes that for everything existent there is something which is the cause of existence and of goodness and of every perfection, for perfection is to exist in the fullest way.

St Thomas' fifth and final way is the so-called 'Teleological Argument' about guiding things to an end. He says that we observe that things in nature act for an end: acorns turn into oak trees, and hydrangeas on acid soil produce blue, not pink, flowers. Things either direct themselves or they are directed by another. Since it cannot be by chance that things in nature often work in the same way and turn out for the better, it must be intended. So things which have no knowledge of their end are directed to it by an Intelligence. Only minds *intend* things. Thomas compares the working of nature and a mind directing natural things to their end with the flight of an arrow and the archer who gives it its aim. For St Thomas the world is neither due to chance nor to necessity but to the intention of someone.

St Thomas thought that there is only one world; he would have had little time for talk about 'other universes'. The order of the universe manifests its unity, he says. It is one because everything in it is ordered by a single order.[8] Binary stars, for example, show us that the law of gravity extends beyond our solar system and, we may suppose, throughout the universe. It is materialists who do not think that the world comes from a mind giving it order, he says, who think that there are many worlds. If there were many, they might clash with one another.

That the world has order means that it is a rational universe. Unless it were a rational universe we would not discover laws of nature at work in it. It is because there are laws of nature that we are able to give some account of how natural things act. All created things have been made with reason because they have been made according to the ideas (*rationes*) of them in the divine Word or Logos. 'Logos' in Greek means both a 'word'

---

[8] *Ibid.* I 47, 1 ad 3.

and a 'reason' for something. The very order of the universe manifests the wisdom of its Maker, as a work of art reflects something of the artist who made it since it comes from a conception in the mind of the artist. St Thomas says that creation may be compared with God as an artefact with the artisan who makes it. Thus we can know that the Creator exists from his creation.

To know that God exists does not, however, mean that we know his 'act of existing', that is what it is for God to exist, as we know the existence of cowslips, say, in a meadow, since we cannot say how God exists; rather only how he does not exist. But we can know that the statement 'God exists' is true.[9]

But when it comes to knowing *what* God is we are as blind as owls in the light of the sun, he says. Nevertheless, with our inquiring minds we naturally desire to know the causes of and reasons for things. Our questioning will eventually take us back to the first cause of everything. However, our minds do not come to rest until we know *what* a thing is. Thus the natural desire to know the causes of things leads us back to the First Cause of all things but it will only come to rest when we see the essence of God. St Thomas would say that man naturally desires to see God and that since a natural desire would not be implanted in us in vain, it is unlikely that it is not meant to be fulfilled in some way, which he says is in the vision of God, which is everlasting beatitude. However, we cannot come to it in this life since it completely transcends the limits of our minds in our present state. Our lasting happiness, he says, will lie in an activity of the highest faculty in us, the intellect, since no desire bears us up so loftily (*tam in sublime*) as the desire of understanding the truth.[10]

[9]*Ibid.* I 3, 4 ad 2.
[10]*Contra Gentiles* III c. 50.

3

———

Analogy

We find some basis for saying that we speak about God by analogy in Scripture itself, since the word 'analogically' (*analogos*) is used in the very passage which says that the existence of the Creator can be known from his creation: 'from the magnitude and beauty of created things their begetter can be considered by analogy' (*Wisdom* 13, 5). St Thomas draws his doctrine of analogy from the *Divine Names* of Pseudo-Dionysius, whose question there is: What knowledge of God do our names for him give us, and how do they express anything about God when his being is altogether above anything which we know of? His answer is that the knowledge they give us of him is not as he is but as he is the source and cause of the perfections in created things, which are like rays diffused from the source of light. Discussion of the names of God goes back to Moses' question at the burning bush, 'What is your name?' (*Exodus* 3, 14).

St Thomas says that we know two things about God: that he is the cause of everything and that he differs from everything caused by him.[1] These two things correspond with the two ways in which we can talk about God: the way of eminence, as he exceeds anything we can know about him from creatures, and the way of negation, as he is not one of other things. We speak of him in the negative way when we say he is *in*finite, *im*mense, *in*visible, which is being not visible etc. This is saying what he is *not*. It is because of these negations that God is

———

[1] *Summa* I 12, 12.

incomprehensible. When we describe how one thing differs from another we narrow it down and define it by setting limits to the way it exists: 'with spots' narrows down a panther to a leopard, for instance. With God, however, it works the other way round; when we say how he differs from other things we only remove limits from the way he exists, as his nature is not confined but unlimited.[2] Thus the negative way is called the *via remotionis*, the way of taking away, or removing, limits from God. For God does not come within any class of things. The only class of thing to which God might belong is being but being is not a class since the only difference from being is non-being, which is not anything at all. It is because these differences of God from other things do not specify divine nature but only remove limitations of existence from him that we cannot say what God is. However, the way of removing should not make us think that God is utterly remote or distant from us; it means rather that he is not one of other things.

We can, however, speak about God positively too, when we call him good, merciful, just. This is by analogy since God is not wise in the same way as a man is because wisdom is a quality in Solomon but is not a quality in God; he *is* wisdom. Thomas discusses analogy under the names of God: these refer to the attributes of God: his goodness, wisdom, power, justice etc. As Shakespeare says of mercy, 'It is an attribute to God himself'.[3] Words can be used in three ways: univocally, equivocally and analogically. Univocally, when we apply a word to several things in the same sense. If our words about God were meant univocally, we would reduce him to the level of created things, making him exist in the same way as they do. In equivocation we use the same word in two quite different senses. If our words about God were only equivocal, we could not say anything meaningful about him, and it would be as well to be silent about him. Yet we would expect to be able to speak about the God who has spoken to us. There is a third way between these two: of analogy with things which, though they differ essentially, are alike in some respect. We use analogy when we describe a

---

[2] *Contra Gentiles* I c. 14.
[3] *The Merchant of Venice* IV 1.

piece of music as 'colourful' because it has a similar effect on us as a colourful painting, thinking perhaps of a Matisse. The term 'chromatic scales' in music is an analogy since notes do not have colour but this effect is produced by playing all the semitones on keys of both colours on a piano. It is analogy too when we talk about 'the ring of truth' since truth does not make a sound, as the ring of a bell does, but when someone is speaking the truth it sounds as if he is because all that he says is consonant. Anything untrue strikes us like a false note.

God can be named in two ways: by analogy proper and by metaphor. There is a difference between calling God goodness, justice, wisdom on the one hand, which is with abstract words, and a rock, a shield, a lamp on the other, which is with concrete words. We distinguish between *how* a word signifies and *what* it signifies.[4] In analogy *how* a word signifies is as it applies to creatures since we know them first and we name him from them. But *what* it signifies applies first to God since he is the source of all perfections which we find in creatures. Thus St Thomas says that all analogy implies the relation of cause.[5] How a word signifies is the way we apprehend the perfection it signifies as we find it in creatures. With metaphor, however, it is the other way round: *how* a word signifies is as it is applied to God when we call him a lamp, for instance, but *what* it signifies is the thing itself since God is not a lamp but a lamp is a lamp.

St Thomas says that we can only name God from things which we do know, which is from created things. The many names of God do not mean that he is not simple but we use many names of him because his perfections, which are one in him, are represented by the great variety of things in creation. A work of art represents an idea of its maker: the Pietà, for example, is a representation in marble of a conception of Michelangelo. Every likeness of God is inadequate since nothing can adequately represent the divine nature, except the divine Word himself. The many names of God doe not mean that he is composite like creatures, because his attributes are only distinct in our minds but are one in reality, since God is his

[4]*Summa* I 13, 13.
[5]*Ibid.* I 5, 2 ad 1.

wisdom, his power, etc. The diverse names of God do not stem from any diversity in him but from the diversity of perfections we find in creatures, which derive from him as their source. Nonetheless, the divine attributes are not synonomous: they do not have the same meaning (sense), though they mean (stand for) one and the same thing in God.

We name God from creatures as the cause of the perfections which we find in them by the 'eminent' way because whatever exists in them exists in God in a far higher way than we can express. God's perfections exist in him in a higher way because they are not distinct from his nature: God is not just living but is Life himself. Even when we speak positively about God, everything we affirm of him can be denied of him in that it does not apply to him as it is found in created things.[6] When we call God good we do not mean that he is good like other things but in a far higher (more eminent) way.

Although we name him after creatures our words signify him better than them because wisdom is a property of a wise man but God *is* wisdom. A wise man *has* wisdom but God *is* the things which other things have. Properly speaking, we cannot predicate things of God since predication introduces complexity, whereas God simply is the things we predicate of him. With God the 'is' of predication is identical with the 'is' of identity. In 'the king is wise' I use the 'is' of predication. In 'Mercury is the nearest planet to the sun' I use the 'is' of identity, since Mercury and the nearest planet to the sun name one and the same thing. To say God is wise is the same as to say he is wisdom. It is for this reason that the divine attributes are names of God. We name someone by an attribute when, for instance, we call Alfonso X of Castile 'the Wise'.

The first analogy there is between God and creatures is that of being, simply as they are existent. We speak by analogy here since God is Being and they share in being. They are not Being but are beings; God is not a being but is Being. 'Whatever has existence and is not existence itself is an existent (a being) by participation.'[7] The idea of participation comes from Plato

[6] *De Divinis Nominibus* V lect. 3.
[7] *Summa* I 3, 4.

and is blended by St Thomas into his Aristotelian philosophy. Plato says that all beautiful things participate in beauty; they are beautiful by sharing in beauty. Plato tells us that he was not just interested in knowing beautiful things but in coming to know beauty itself, which he said is the cause of beauty in beautiful things. Beauty itself is the very idea of beauty. Likewise, things are sheep because they share in the idea, or form, of sheep. The real things for Plato are the Ideas since they have their being unchangingly, whereas all the changing things we see in this world, such as sheep, share in non-being as well as in being since they come into and go out of existence and cease to be what they were by changing. We might express it like this: oysters come into and go out of existence but the idea of oyster remains constant. The major difference between Aristotle and Plato is that Aristotle held that the forms of things do not exist on their own, as Plato supposed, but in the things of which they are the form. In Aquinas participation means first of all that things participate in being because they receive their existence.

Other things are not Being but beings because they receive their existence from another. For things to share in existence we must come back to some being which does not receive its existence from another but is its own existence. St Thomas tells us that this thought comes from Avicenna.[8] Everything which shares in existence ultimately gets its existence from something which does not share in existence, otherwise it would be like one of them having another source of its existence, but which is Existence itself. Thus this thing exists in a wholly other way than all other things. When we say that God is Being we do not mean that he is part of the being of things, which would be pantheism and to give the incommunicable name to stones and stocks.[9] He is 'the infinite sea of being', a phrase which is found in St John Damascene (c. 675-749) and is echoed by Dante:

> *onde si muovono a diversi porti*
> *per lo gran mar dell'essere*[10]

[8]*De Potentia* q. 3 art. 5.
[9]*Wisdom* 14, 21.
[10]*Paradiso* I 112-113.

Whence they move to various harbours through the great sea of being. Other things have existence but God is existence.

God is also his essence since he is the divine nature, as he is wisdom, power etc., as well as his existence. God's essence and existence are identical because he has not received his existence from anything else. The doctrine of the identity of essence and existence in God has been criticized for making it look as though God's essence is that there is a God. That there is such a thing is not part of the essence of anything. We distinguish between the essence and existence of things because I can know what a dodo is, which is the essence of a dodo, without knowing whether any dodos exist. The existence of Columbus and his essence, or nature, are not identical since Columbus is not human nature, or humanity, and so for Columbus to be a man and to be the individual man that he was are not the same thing. But unless God's essence and existence are identical, he is not his existence but shares in being, which he gets from something else, which would then be the cause of it in him. As Aquinas points out, that everything which participates in existence by receiving it goes back to something which is existence itself is connected with the simplicity of God. The simplicity of God means that he is his existence, his understanding, his blessedness and so on, and that he is identical with his attributes since he is goodness, wisdom, life etc. Existence is not something which comes to his divine nature. Thus the divine name which was told to Moses, 'Who is', is the most appropriate name of God since it signifies existence itself.

4

Creation

When St Thomas is discussing creation and the origin of the world, he is not considering how one kind of thing came from another but what is common to all the things there are in the universe, which is simply that they have existence. This leads us to ask about the cause of all existence. Thus he calls creation 'the emanation of the whole of existence'.[1] This is not to be taken as a series of emanations from God but to mean that God is the cause of all existence. When Thomas says that all being comes from one universal cause, he is opposing the idea of Avicenna, and others before him, that there is a chain of intelligences, the first of which was produced by God and which in turn produced the next and so on, going down to the one which made the material world. Thomas' point is that God creates everything immediately, and not by means of other intelligences or heavenly beings. He adopts a proposition of the eleventh century *Liber de Causis* (Book on Causes), which Thomas was the first to identify as a selection from the fifth century Platonist writer, Proclus: 'the first of all created things is existence'. Existence is the first of created things because presupposed to any making in the world is the existence of things, and creation means that something rather than nothing exists.

The first effect of all is the existence of things since nothing in the world causes an effect without something else already existing. When we make something we presuppose the existence of other things: of paints, brushes and paper to produce a

[1] *Summa* I 45, 1.

painting, for example, and these presuppose the natural things from which they are made: wood, minerals or pigments, sable hair and so on. We make things out of already existent things but God did not require the existence of anything else to make the world. When we, or natural things, make things, we produce form in matter but God produces the whole thing from scratch, so to speak. Creation is the production of the total being of a thing. A glassblower produces glasses out of molten glass but God did not produce the existence of the world in anything else. Properly speaking, creation is to make out of nothing; that is, the world was not created out of anything existent, but only *by* something existent. It is to produce both the object and that from which it is made together all at once. Creatures can only bring new things into existence by drawing out what is potential in something already existent, as a carving is made out of a block of wood, but there was nothing which was potentially the world before God made it. When we make things there is our action and something which receives our action, as a lump of silver receives the beating action of a silversmith in the making of a brooch. But in the making of things out of other things we eventually come back to just making, which is pure action, for at creation there was nothing to receive this action. Only God can do this kind of action, since he is sheer actuality.

Only God can create because clearly things which have received their existence from another cannot produce existence, which is presupposed to all other making. The power of any creature is finite since it has received its existence but creation requires infinite power, since the distance between non-existence and existence is infinite. It is greater than the distance between any created things, between a snail and a star, which at least have existence in common, just as they are beings. Creation is to produce existence absolutely — 'the first of all created things is existence'. Only God can create because the first effect presupposed to all other effects is existence, which is the effect of the First Cause alone.

God not only creates the universe but continually keeps it in existence. He is not like a watchmaker who, having wound up the clock of the universe, lets it run its course without any more attention to the machine he has set in motion. However, this does not mean that divine intervention is needed from time to time to restore the equilibrium of the universe when the anomalies which exist in the motions of some of the planets become too great, as Newton thought. Laplace showed that these discrepancies are self-regulating; so when he presented the first part of his *Traitè de Mécanique Céleste* to Napoleon, who asked him why he had left out any mention of the Creator, he replied 'I have no need of that hypothesis'. Aquinas might have agreed with Laplace that the intervention of God is not needed but not that we have no need of the hypothesis of the Creator for the world to remain in existence, since it continually depends on that power through which it has existence at all. Remove the cause and there is no effect; take away the source of power and the light goes out. God is the cause of all action since other things only act because they have existence, which comes from him. But God does not cause everything immediately; he makes other things be natural causes. Other things can only be causes in virtue of the First Cause, since things only exist because of it. God preserves the universe in existence by the same action as he brought it into existence. The conservation of the world is not by some new action but by a continuation of the action by which he gives existence, as the conservation of light in the air is by a continued influx of light from the sun, the source of light. Everything requires God to sustain it in existence, as air requires the sun every moment to be light.[2]

In St Thomas' view of the world, God is active throughout the universe. His presence in it is an *active* presence. He is both in all things as the cause of everything and above all things since the way in which he exists is altogether other than theirs. God is in all things in three ways: by his presence, his essence and his power. By his presence, as all things are in his sight and are present to him. By his essence, since he is the cause of everything existing externally to himself (but he is not the essence of anything, as pantheism holds). And by his power directing and sustaining everything. The third way, by his

[2] *Ibid.* I 104, 1 ad 4.

power, also includes God's providence ruling the world and excludes the opinion of the Manichees that there are some things which are not subject to God but to a contrary principle of evil. God works intimately in all things, giving them existence since existence is the most interior, the core of all things. Existence, Aquinas says, is the deepest and inmost of everything existent in reality.[3]

[3]*Ibid.* I 8, 1.

5

Evil

We find some of St Thomas' deepest insights into existence in his writing on evil. It is perhaps no accident that Thomas gave so much thought to the matter of evil since he was a member of an order which grew out of a preaching mission of its founder, St Dominic, to the Albigenses who held the Manichean heresy, around 1205. To talk about evil you also have to talk about good, just as you cannot talk about numbers and only talk about the number nought.

Against the teaching of the Manichees that the material world is evil and the work of a malevolent being, St Thomas affirms the intrinsic goodness of creation. All being is good in itself since it comes from God. Creation is good because the world is not due to necessity but to the will of God, who freely created it since, being perfect, he does not need or depend on other things for his good.[1] The end of all things is the good since everything seeks its good. Nothing in the world is its own end since everything in it shares in goodness. Nothing created is its own good since it has an end beyond itself. God is the last end of everything since he does not act for an end beyond himself; if he did, that end would transcend him. God does not act *for* an end but solely *out of* his goodness. As Thomas says, the only end God can be said to act for is to *communicate* his goodness.[2] In seeking its own good everything seeks God since the perfections of created things are likenesses of the perfection of God, from whom they derive. Thomas would say that

---

[1] *Summa* I 104, 3 ad 2.
[2] *Ibid.* I 44, 4 ad 1.

nothing is good except by sharing in some likeness of God, however faint it may be.

As evil is the opposite of good, and all being is good in itself, so evil turns out to be the opposite of being, that is non-being. A being is something which actually exists as distinct from being merely potential. This is the substantial existence of a thing, or its being a substance, that is an individual thing. A penny, for instance, has substantial existence and is potentially a bent or corroded penny. Each thing is called a 'being', St Thomas says, simply because of its substantial existence.[3] In the first chapter of *De Ente et Essentia,* he gives two meanings of being (*ens*): (1) as we predicate things of something existent: what it is as a whole, which is substance, its shape, quantity, position, what it is doing or having done to it, etc. And (2) as being signifies the truth of a proposition. Evil, for instance blindness, only has being in this second sense, as something is blind but not as blindness is anything in itself. We can perhaps record a shift in St Thomas' thinking while he was in Paris since, when he came to explain being in almost identical terms a few years later, he replaces *ens* (being) with *esse* (existence) and says that *esse* has two senses: the actuality of an existent thing inasmuch as it is a being, which is that by which it is called something in nature. This *esse* is attributed to things in two ways: as something really has existence or *is,* which is a substance existing in itself; and to everything which does not exist in itself but in another. In this way whiteness, for instance, does not have being by itself but is that by which something is white. The second sense of *esse* is the verbal copula and this sort of 'is' is not in the nature of things but in the mind affirming or negating things. This sort of *esse* can be attributed to everything about which it is possible to make a proposition.[4] Blindness is not anything in the nature of things, since we do not call things blind which are not meant by nature to see, but we can say that something is blind. Blindness is an evil in things which are meant to see since it is the lack of an activity which belongs to

---

[3] *Ibid.* I 5, 1 ad 1.
[4] *Quodlibet* IX 2, 3 (Advent 1257).

its proper and complete existence. Thus evil is not anything existent; rather it is a defect or the diminishment of something's existence. Evil is the *privation* of being as it is also the privation of good. For things are not worse by participating more in evil, as they are better by sharing more in goodness, but by a greater deprivation of good.

There is not a principle of evil as there is a principle of good, since evil is not anything existent in itself. All good things come from one cause but evil is due to many defects. All good things point to a single source, like radii converging at their centre, but evil points away, or recedes, in any direction. Likewise, truth unifies since truth is consistent, but falsehood disperses since there is a discrepancy in untrue things. There is no dissension among good things since they are consonant with one another like the instruments of an orchestra, which are all in tune and in time with one another, though they have different parts to play.

If there were a contrary principle of evil, the universe would not have the order it does since the two principles would be at war with one another. Only good can cause or produce things since evil is not anything existent and only existent things can be causes. Evil rather harms and destroys things. If evil were anything existent, either God would be the cause of evil as he is the source of all existence, or he would not be the sole cause of existence since there would be another principle of being besides him. There is not a principle of evil, as there is a principle of good, since anything which were totally evil would be totally non-existent. A principle of evil would be evil by nature but nothing desires what is contrary to its nature but what is like it. Though things naturally desire their good, anything which were evil by its nature would be unable to desire good, since this would be a contradiction for it. St Thomas thus produces many arguments against the Manichean view that the source of the world's existence is an evil principle. A principle of evil would consume itself, as evil is destructive of existence, since evil is the privation of existence and total evil is the total negation of anything's existence. But you cannot negate nought. Evil is like a parasite which destroys itself by consuming the very thing on which it depends for existence, as ivy will eventually wither when it has killed the tree on which it lived.

Since there is nothing that is evil in itself, it follows that evil is only found in something which is good, at least inasmuch as it has being. Evil presupposes good since it does not have any existence by itself. Nothing is naturally or essentially bad. Even the bad angels were created good. Yet we see many things in nature which are evil for those who suffer them, for the minnow which is swallowed by the pike. St Thomas' view is that whatever preserves the order of nature, as animals kill to preserve their existence, is the good of nature. What is evil for individuals is the good of the species but it is otherwise with beings, such as ourselves, who have a perpetual end. Then it is not just the good of the species but of the individual which matters.

The cause of evil is not a principle of evil since no one chooses evil for its own sake, such as harming someone, but for the sake of some good, such as possessing their gold ring, because, as Aquinas observes, evil does not have the aspect of an end. If everything seeks its own good, whence then comes evil? The belief of the Manichees was that it comes from an evil being. St Thomas was determined to scotch this heresy. Evil does not come from the author of creation, since evil is not anything created, not being anything existent. Nor can nature be the source of evil since evil is against nature and nature often acts in the same way; so, if nature were the cause of evil, evil would be from necessity and things would be unalterably evil. If evil sprang from necessity, virtuous actions would be necessary too and there would not be any true virtue, which is voluntary. St Thomas argues then that evil neither comes from the Creator of the world nor from nature but from something which acts in an indeterminate and variable way, which is wills. Evil lies in desiring what is good here and now but which is not ordered by reason. Sin, he says, either lies in a discord with right reason or with divine law.

> Take but degree away, untune that string,
> And, hark! what discord follows.[5]

[5] *Triolus and Cressida* Act I sc. iii.

It might seem, however, that since original sin is inherited with the nature that is passed on to each one of us, nature is the cause of evil. This is not so because the flaw in human nature is not itself due to nature in the first instance but to the will and fault of the first man. Original sin was an actual sin of Adam. The disorder in human nature as we receive it has fault, or guilt, from the will of its source. Original sin is transmitted by generation, not first by imitating Adam, because we are all parts of human nature. Thus St Thomas calls original sin 'the sin of nature', as distinct from actual sin. As human nature is passed on by generation, so is the sin of nature. As original justice, which consisted in the harmony of human nature with appetite ordered to reason and the mind to God, was given to Adam as a gift of grace to pass on to his posterity, so the loss of it in his descendents is a kind of injustice.

It appears that God is the cause of sin since he is the cause of all actions. However, he is not the cause of what is sinful about them since sin, St Thomas says, does not have an effective but *defective* cause. When God is said to harden Pharoah's heart, he seems to be the cause of evil too. Nonetheless, God does not cause moral blindness but is only said to harden people's hearts in that he leaves them to what they deserve and witholds from them his grace, which he gives to whom he wills, otherwise it would/be his grace.[6] It is solely in his mercy that *not* God works in the hearts of men to incline their wills to the good. God does not cause hardness of heart anymore than the sun is the cause of darkness in a room the shutters of which are closed when it is day. The sun shines by necessity of nature but God enlightens minds voluntarily and freely, otherwise it would not be a free gift. Sin is aversion from God, a turning away from that light which never turns away itself. God does not make anyone sin since he only wills the good.

When we are talking about voluntary actions, Thomas divides evil into two sorts: the evil of fault and the evil of punishment. One could say that God causes the evil of punishment but not directly, since there is only punishment because of something which God does not will, namely sin. God only wills the pain of

[6]*In Romanos* c. IX lect. 3.

punishment because he wills justice, which is the good of the whole of society and a higher good than that an individual wrong-doer should not suffer pain. The pain of punishment is an evil for the individual but for a higher good, the order of justice. Thus the guilt of sin is a greater evil than the pain of punishment, since it is turning away from the highest good. St Thomas goes against an age which thinks that pain is a greater evil than the loss of grace. The evil of guilt is greater than the evil of pain because we are responsible for guilt, which inheres in a person and separates from God. The greatest evil is not pain but to be separated from the ultimate good, which is God. It is a greater evil not to shun doing evil or to think that what is evil is not evil than it is to suffer pain. St Thomas also goes counter to the utilitarian attitude of the present time, which assesses actions by the greater number to whom it is supposed they will bring benefit and thus countenances evil that good may come. Thus any means might be justified by a certain end, if it was thought that a detriment to many people could be avoided by wronging an innocent person. As St Thomas says, evil harms the doer in the very doing of it since it makes his will bad.[7]

---

[7] *Summa* I 48, 5 ad 4.

6

The Trinity

There are certain things which reason by itself could never know about God because reason on its own only knows about God from creatures as the Creator. The mind of man could never have conceived of God as a Trinity of equal persons but only one God. God is one does not mean that there is one God rather than several but that God is not divided. 'God' is a natural name since we can ask whether there are several gods or one God; but Father, Son and Holy Spirit are proper or personal names of God, which have been revealed to us.

The doctrine of the Trinity is nowhere stated as such in Scripture; rather it follows from the realization that in the New Testament the Father, Son and Holy Spirit are all spoken of as God. How each one is God is consistent with the revelation in the Old Testament, taken over in the New, that God is one was something which the early Church had to work out. This she did especially in the fourth century, when she established her doctrine at two Councils by declaring the Son to be of the same being as, that is 'consubstantial' with, the Father at Nicea in 325, and the Holy Spirit to be adored and glorified with the Father and the Son as God at Constantinople in 381. We see the beginning of this reflection in the Gospel of St John, in which Jesus makes plain that God who is spoken of in the Old Testament is his Father and promises to send the Holy Spirit, who proceeds from the Father. However, we find some foreshadowing of the Trinity already in the Old Testament, which speaks of God's creative word and spirit.[1]

---

[1] E.g. *Psalms* 33, 6; 104, 30; 148, 5.

27

There are two main approaches to the Trinity. One, which is known as the 'economic' Trinity, begins with the revelation of the Trinity through the course of the Old and New Testaments. For the Trinity was not revealed all at once but gradually, especially with the sending of the Son and the Holy Spirit as told in the New Testament. The other approach starts with the doctrine given as a whole and is known as the 'immanent' Trinity because it considers God in himself rather than as he came to be known gradually in the course of saving history. In recent times, there has been a return to the economic Trinity, which is the way St Augustine begins his great work on the Trinity, going through all the passages referring to the Father, Son and Holy Spirit in the first four books. St Thomas, however, adopts the approach of the immanent Trinity, though, if we do want the Scriptural texts for the Trinity, we will find them given by him copiously in the opening section of Book Four of his *Summa contra Gentiles*. It should be said for the immanent Trinity that there surely is a place for considering God in himself, since eternal life will consist in doing just this and the Trinity is the fountain of all the other mysteries of the Christian faith, as the source of the sending of the Son and Holy Spirit to redeem and sanctify us is their processions in God. Part of the task of any account of the Trinity is an attempt to understand the *unity* of the Father, Son and Holy Spirit, so that they are seen to be not three Gods but one, in which the mystery lies.

St Thomas starts with the processions rather than relations in God, thus reversing the order of St Augustine's inquiry, since he says that the relations arise from the processions. For God to be one, the divine nature must have a single source. Thus there is only one Unbegotten, who is not from another. If there are others in God, they must proceed in some way. For a divine person to proceed from the Father and at the same time to be of the same nature, the procession cannot result in anything external to or diverse from its source. Thus the two processions, of the Son and of the Holy Spirit, need to be explained in terms of an activity which does not necessarily result in anything external, and St Thomas finds an analogy for this in thinking, which is an *intrinsic* activity of the mind, since

I can go on thinking without affecting anything outside or around me. The two processions in God correspond with the two activities of the mind: thinking and willing.

The mind is an appropriate image for the Trinity since it is in the mind that we are in the image of God. There is an image of God in us, but since the image is more distant and obscure in irrational creatures it is only called a 'vestige', or trace, of God in them. St Thomas enumerates three ways in which there is an image of God in us: we know ourselves, as God knows and loves himself; we share in intelligent nature; and, thirdly, in thinking of something an interior word, or concept, comes forth in the mind.[2] Elsewhere, he says that there is a representation of the Trinity in the mind as it knows itself and begets its word.[3] St Thomas, then, lays particular emphasis in his view of the image of God on our capacity to form *words*, as God begets his Word.

If we have self-understanding, God certainly understands himself; only far more perfectly than we do ourselves. In thinking of himself God has a perfect conception of his nature, which is his Word. The mind's conception of what it thinks of is a likeness of it; if it were not a likeness it would be a conception of something else. This conception is called by Augustine an inner word, *verbum cordis*. Although we think of words primarily as the sounds we utter, the interior conception of the mind is a word first, since a word signifies an interior conception of the mind. What is in the mind is a prior word, since without this there is nothing for the outer word to express. 'What is in us is not the thing itself but a likeness of it conceived by the intellect, which external sounds signify. Hence the conception is called an interior word, which is signified by an external word'.[4] A concept is a word because I do not know a thing unless I have a word for it. When I see a plant the name of which I do not know, I cannot say which it is but only what it is like with many words. But when I know the word for it I can say what I have in mind in *one* word.

---

[2] *Summa* I 93, 7.
[3] *De Veritate* q. 10 art. 7.
[4] *Contra Gentiles* IV c. 11.

We have many words for the many things there are but God says everything with one Word, since in thinking of himself he thinks of all other things too in his Word. We have one thought of one thing and a different thought of another thing but God has only one Word since he thinks of all things in one act of thinking. God makes everything by his Word since he thinks of everything in his Word, just as a craftsman makes things according to a conception in his mind of the thing he makes. Thus the Word is called by Augustine 'the art of God', *ars dei*.[5] When the Word is referred to God, he is the Image of God, since he is the perfectly adequate likeness of his nature. When he is referred to created things, the Word is the exemplar of everything which God makes, just as the conception, or word, in the mind of the artist is the exemplar of the work of art he produces. The Word is the exemplar of all God makes since in thinking of himself God thinks of all other things too.

The procession of the Word in God is called generation because generation begets a likeness in the same nature, and the word which comes forth in God's understanding of himself is a complete likeness of his nature. Begetting, or generation, is for something to come forth, or proceed, from a living source as a likeness of it. The Word begotten is God because God's understanding and existence are identical; understanding is not anything additional to his existing, since it is not something he does intermittently but is always doing. Our ideas are not identical with our minds since we do not actually have at once all the ideas we are capable of having. Our understanding is not identical with our existence; so what is in our minds is not of the same nature. But since God's understanding is his existence, his Word is not accidental to him but belongs to his nature. My understanding is not my existence. Since God's understanding and existence are identical, his understanding of himself, which is his Word, is a subsistent thing, that is God. The Son who is begotten is called the Word rather than the Thought of God since, properly speaking, God does not go from one thought to another, as we do, but simply contemplates the truth all in one, as though in a single *coup d'oeil*. The whole

[5] *De Trinitate* VI 10.

Trinity is spoken by the Word, as the Father in thinking of himself thinks of the Son and of the Holy Spirit also.[6]

When the Son is said to be generated, or begotten, by the Father, the Father communicates the whole of his nature, not just a part of himself. Procession in God means this communication of divine nature.[7] The divine nature is wholly in the Son as it is communicated by generation, and in the Holy Spirit as it is breathed forth. The Father is in the Son because the whole of his nature is in the Son, and the Son is in the Father as in the source of his divine nature. The Son remains in the Father, though he comes forth from him, as a word proceeds yet remains within the mind.

Although the Son who is begotten in God's understanding of himself is God, the Son does not beget another son in thinking of himself and this son another son and so on, but there is only one Son of God because God thinks of everything in a single act of intuition. God has only one Son since he has only one act of understanding and a perfect concept of himself.

The generation of the Son is not something which happened once and is now over, but God is always begetting his Son as he is always thinking of himself. There never was a time when the Son was not, as Arius said there was; but the Son is eternal with the Father as a word is simultaneous with thinking. Arius made the Son the first of created things by taking the phrase 'the first-born of creation' (*Colossians* 1, 15) literally. If the Son were not of the same nature as God but created, he would be made out of nothing and we would not say that he is 'God from God, Light from Light', which is to be from something, not from nothing. St Paul explains in the next verse that he is called 'the first-born of creation' since everything was made through him. St Thomas takes up this point: the Son is the first-born of creation because he is begotten as the principle of all created things, which were made through him. He is the first-born not because he is the first *of* creatures but because he is *before* all creatures.[8] Arius is forestalled by St John since, if the Son were

[6]*Summa* I 34, 1 ad 3.
[7]*Ibid.* I 27, 3 ad 2.
[8]*In Colossos* c. 1 lect. 4.

created, it would not be true that 'there is not anything which has come into existence which has not come into existence through him' (*John* 1, 3), since there would be something which came to be which did not come to be through him, namely himself.

The Father is the principle of the Son but not the cause of the Son, since nothing in God is caused. How then can one and the same divine nature be unbegotten in the Father and begotten in the Son? St Thomas' answer is that the divine essence does not beget but the Father begets the Son. The essence is a begetting thing in the Father and a begotten thing in the Son: the essence is not *generans* but it is a *res generans* in the Father.[9]

The divine Word is not some merely abstract concept but a word which breathes forth, or inspires, love: *verbum autem dei Patris est spirans amorem*.[10] The procession of the will in God is not called generation because love does not beget a likeness of its object but is an inclination towards it. Thus the one who proceeds by way of the will loving is called the Spirit since love impels one towards what is loved, as a wind impels things. In Hebrew the same word, *ruah*, means a wind and a spirit. The Holy Spirit proceeds from the Father and the Son because their love is mutual. The mutual love of the Father and the Son is a subsistent relation which proceeds from within, as his understanding of himself is. As God's loving is identical with his existence, so what proceeds in God as his loving is God also. The Father loves the Son, and us too St Thomas adds, by the Holy Spirit; not as though the Holy Spirit were the principle of his loving but as the Spirit is love proceeding.[11] The Holy Spirit does not proceed *from* the love of the Father and the Son but *is* the love proceeding from the Father and the Son. He proceeds as their mutual love. The Father remains the sole fountain of the godhead, though the Holy Spirit proceeds from two, because the Son only has it from the Father that he breathes forth the Spirit. The Father and the Son have all

---

[9] *Summa* I 39, 5 ad 5.
[10] Augustine, *De Trinitate* IX 10.
[11] *Summa* I 37, 2 ad 3.

things in common which do not distinguish them *vis-à-vis* one another: 'all that the Father has is mine' (*John* 16, 15). One of these things is breathing forth the Holy Spirit. Thus there is only one source of the godhead.

Although we might not think of the Spirit as a person, as we think the Father and the Son are, the Holy Spirit is clearly spoken of as God in Scripture in the same way that they are, for he is said to do things which only God does: he searches all things, even the depths of God; he speaks the hidden things of God; he reveals things; he speaks through the prophets; he teaches interiorly; he dwells in us; he is poured out in our hearts; he is everywhere, filling the universe; he creates and he sanctifies us.

The Son and the Holy Spirit are not distinct unless they have a relation to one another as well as to the Father. They only have this if they differ in their origin, not in the source but in the *way* that they proceed from their source. If they both proceed from the Father alone they are not distinct in their relation. Thus one of them has to come from the other as well as from the Father. This is the Holy Spirit since love proceeds from knowledge, for nothing is loved unless it is known, as love often grows with a deeper knowledge of another person in human relationships. Also it is the Son who is said to send the Holy Spirit who proceeds from the Father, and to breathe the Holy Spirit on the Apostles when he is risen.

The only distinction in God is of origin and opposite relation; otherwise each divine person is all that the other two are. The divine relations are internal because they arise from internal actions, of understanding and willing. There is opposite relation where there is a distinction of origin, as one is the source of another or comes from another. The Father is the source of the divine nature in that he does not have it from another; the Son has it from another and the Holy Spirit from two others. That there are relations in God is implied by the words, 'the Word was *with* God', the proposition indicating relation. The relations in God are *real* relations, otherwise God would not really be the Father, Son and Holy Spirit, as Sabellius thought, saying that they were merely aspects of God. Thus the divine relations are subsistent things (*res*, from which we get

our word 'real'), since they do not come to divine nature but
are identical with it. It is because the relations are identical with
the divine nature that they are subsistent things. Divine
fatherhood *is* the Father, 'from whom all fatherhood takes its
name' (*Ephesians* 3, 14); and divine sonship *is* the Son. These
relations constitute the divine persons, as a person means
something subsisting in intelligent nature. Person in God
signifies a relation as a subsistent thing in divine nature and
this, St Thomas says, is for there to be several persons in God.[12]

The use of 'person' when talking about God has become
questionable today, partly because of the more psychological
conception of person as an individual who determines him or
herself by free choice. Though God is three persons, he does
not have three wills, for instance, but one. However, it would
be strange not to think of God, who is love, as personal. Calling
God 'personal' does not mean that he is one person, for he is
three persons. 'Person' helps us to grasp that God is someone
we can relate to. It would not be the same for the Father, Son
and Holy Spirit to be called three 'X's' or three 'Y's' instead of
three 'persons', as some suggest, since X and Y stand for
impersonal objects but Father, Son and Holy Spirit do not
name three X's or three Y's since they are *proper* and personal
names.

Whatever the difficulties are about using 'person' for God,
it is worth recalling that we owe the very concept of person to
the fourth century debate about the Trinity, in which it was
wrought, since the ancients before then only had a very meagre
conception of person. St Thomas acknowledges some of these
difficulties himself: for instance, person among human beings
means an individual substance but not so in God, since God is
not three substances. 'Substance' is the exact equivalent for
'hypostasis' (literally, standing under), which was being used
in the East for 'person', but 'substance' was used in the West for
the divine nature. Thomas tells us why person came to be used
in speaking of God: it was as though forced to do so, he says,
since Eunomius was using 'hypostasis', the Greek word for the
persons, not in the sense of subsistent thing but of substance,

[12]*Summa* I 30, 1.

making them three Gods (tritheism); so another word had to be found. This was 'person'. St Thomas adopts Boethius' standard definition of person, 'an individual substance of rational nature', but by introducing two slight but significant changes he renders it more suitable for the Trinity: 'a person is an individual subsisting in intellectual nature',[13] thus avoiding three persons being three substances in God and because, strictly speaking, God does not have rational nature, since he has no need to reason about things, as we do, but he has intelligent nature. One of the main aspects of the modern concept of person was just as much part of the medieval concept since individual only applies to God, Thomas says, as it signifies the incommunicability of a person.[14] 'Incommunicability' means that one person is not another but that Father, Son and Holy Spirit are distinct.

Thomas regarded it as fitting to apply person to God since person signifies the highest thing we know of existing in nature. Since individuals are found in a more perfect way in rational beings than among other creatures, they have a special name. But we use 'person' of God by analogy, since it is said of God in a higher way; 'person' signifies that which is most perfect in nature, namely subsisting in intellectual nature, but it is not said of God in the same way as of creatures but in a more excellent way, since every perfection is to be attributed to God. Sometimes 'what?' asks about a nature, as in 'What is man?' and sometimes about a supposit or subject, as in 'What swims in the sea?' — a fish, a whale or a seal. Person answers the question about this second sort of what.[15] Thomas also points out that that which 'person' signifies is said of God in numerous ways in Scripture, as he is said to make known his word, to be merciful etc.

Although the divine persons are distinct from one another, they are not three Gods but one, since each is God. The divine relations are not distinct from the divine nature but only from one another. God's attributes: his power, wisdom, justice,

---

[13]*De Potentia* q. 9 art. 3.
[14]*Summa* I 29, 3 ad 4.
[15]*Ibid.* I 29, 4 ad 2.

goodness etc. do not constitute persons since they are not opposite to one another, nor do they come from one another, but are common to all three persons. Each divine person is all that either of the other two are since God *is* his wisdom, his power etc. The wisdom of the Father is the same as the wisdom of the Son and of the Holy Spirit. There is unity in God since each of the divine persons is identical with the divine nature. They do not have a relation to the essence, since each *is* the divine nature, but only to one another. There are three supposits of one and the same nature in God since three divine persons do not make three deities, as three men make three humanities. God is his nature but Socrates is not humanity or identical with human nature. Thus three human beings are three instances of human nature, or three humanities, since no one of them is human nature, but divine nature is not instantiated three times in three divine persons, since each is identical with divine nature. As Thomas says, the divine essence is not multiplied by there being three supposits of it because God is his essence.[16] Since essence and existence are identical in God, the divine persons do not have three existences, as three men do, but one.[17] They are as undivided in their existence as they are in their nature. As St Thomas neatly puts it: no one is the other since *to be* the Father (esse Patr*em*) is not to be the Son; but the existence *of* the Father (esse Patr*is*) is the same as the existence of the Son. There is distinction but not division in the Trinity; the godhead exists entire and undivided in each person. If it were divided, they would share in divine nature and so would not be identical with it.

St Thomas does not leave God 'out there', so to speak, as though he were utterly remote from us, but by returning to his starting point of the processions in God he shows how God's understanding and loving of himself are adumbrated in us by the sending of the Son and of the Holy Spirit in us when we know and love God. These are the 'invisible missions' of the Son and Holy Spirit. The divine missions are founded on the interior processions, for only those persons are sent who

[16]*De Potentia* q. 9, 5 ad 13.
[17]*Summa* III 17, 2 ad 3.

proceed; the Father is never said to be sent since he does not come from another. The visible missions were the sending of the Son into the world and the coming down of the Holy Spirit on the Apostles at Pentecost; the invisible missions are interior to us. When God makes his dwelling in us, it is not as though he is in us for the first time, since he is present in all things by his presence, essence and power, but in a new way by grace. We are conformed with God by grace. God is only said to 'dwell' in us; he is not said to dwell in irrational things, which cannot know or love him. Although it only says that the Father and the Son will come to make their dwelling in us (*John* 14, 23), the Holy Spirit is implied too, since where any one of them is there are the other two, since each person is in the other: the Father is in the Son and the Son in the Father and so on.

As the Son proceeds by way of understanding, and the Holy Spirit by the way of loving, we are assimilated to the Son by an enlightenment of the mind (*illuminatio intellectus*) when we love God.[18] Thus the Word inspiring love and love proceeding from knowledge is the pattern of our own knowing and loving. We are made sharers in the divine Word and in love proceeding, St Thomas says, by knowing and loving God.[19] Notable is the way in which Thomas extends the Pauline idea of conformity with Christ to conformity with the Holy Spirit too. We are made like the Holy Spirit by charity, which is poured into us by the Holy Spirit, 'who is the love of the Father and the Son; our participation in this love is charity'.[20] St Thomas, however, differed from the Master of the *Sentences*, Peter Lombard, on the question whether all charity is uncreated grace. St Thomas says, No, since, if it were, charity would not be voluntary in us. The presence of the Holy Spirit in us is uncreated grace, as he is uncreated himself, but the effects of his presence are created grace. The effect of charity is to make us more perfectly in the likeness of the Holy Spirit.[21] Thus the image of God in us is completed by our assimilation to the Holy Spirit.

[18]*Ibid.* I 43, 5 ad 2.
[19]*Ibid.* I 38, 1.
[20]*Ibid.* II-II 24, 2.
[21]*Ibid.* II-II 24, 5 ad 3.

7

The Soul

In his consideration of the human soul, St Thomas is saying what man is. Discounting those in ancient times who thought of the soul as something material, two main views of the soul came down to the Middle Ages: those of Plato and Aristotle. Until the thirteenth century the one best known to Christian thinkers was that of Plato, who however saw the soul as something foreign to the body. Aristotle remedied Plato's lack of the unity of body and soul by making the soul the form of the body, but his difficulty was then to show that the individual soul can survive on its own. It was St Thomas' master, St Albert, who took up seriously Aristotle's writings on the soul. Like Aristotle, Albert was a keen observer of natural and living things. St Thomas himself dispels Plato's dichotomy of the body and soul, which reappeared with Descartes, and emphasizes the essential unity of body and soul. It is *natural* for human souls to be embodied, he maintains. In Plato the body is a hindrance to the soul and the best thing for the soul is to be released from the body. Descartes came to the conclusion that what *I* am is really my soul since he found that he was still aware that he existed even when supposing that he did not have a body; so he thought that what I am is not a body but a conscious being, which he identified with the soul, since it is incorporeal. St Thomas' reply to this would have been: 'If only my soul is saved, *I* am not saved, nor is any other man'.[1] He also says that Peter's soul is not Peter, and when we pray to 'Peter' now we can do so because implicit in our prayer to him is the belief that he will

[1] *In I Corinthos* c. XV lect. 2.

have his body again at the resurrection.[2] Thomas, consistent with this thought that a human being by nature consists of a body and soul, simply denies that the separated soul on its own is a person, since the soul by itself is not the whole of human nature.[3]

Ever since Descartes (1596-1650) the modern concept of soul has been associated with consciousness. 'Conscious' is not a word which occurs much in St Thomas, who thus would not have thought that what persons are is consciousnesses, as is commonly supposed today. Aristotle had a wider concept of soul, which covers all living things. We call living things 'animate' from *anima*, a soul: sea-anemones are animate, pebbles inanimate. The soul is what makes something living. Life is manifest in movement and activity. Plants, which move by growth and inclining to the source of light, have vegetable souls. Plants, however, do not move from place to place but an animal moves itself and has a sensitive soul since it is equipped with senses (except in anomalous cases, such as moles being blind). Human beings have rational souls, since thinking is one of their vital activities. Other animals are not rational like men since, though they may look for things not present to them and so are not altogether confined to objects before their senses (squirrels know when it is time to store nuts and swallows when to fly southwards before winter approaches), and may be taught in experiments to distinguish between geometrical shapes, they will never be able to do geometry, since this involves having certain *concepts*.

However, a man does not have three souls, though he has the powers of all three kinds of soul, but one soul since what gives something its unity is that it has one substantial form. That we do not have several souls but one was one of the points in St Thomas, for which he was posthumously condemned by Bishop Tempier in Paris in 1277, though the condemnation was not made public in the end. The main objection to holding that we have one soul was a theological one, since it seemed to imply that Christ's body in the tomb had no form since it was

[2]*Summa* II-II 83, 11 ad 5.
[3]*Ibid.* I 29, 1 ad 5.

without the soul in death. So some said that the corpse of Christ had a form of corporeity, which made it a body. St Thomas, however, saw no need to invoke an additional form of corporeity to give the body its bodiliness, since for him it is the human soul which makes a body be a human body and the body without its soul is not even a human body. It is no longer a human being, for instance. So St Thomas was not perturbed to say that Christ's body in the tomb was not the same *man* as hung on the cross, though it was the same *person* since his body remained united to the same person of the Word in death, as did his soul too separately.[4]

Body and soul are not two things with no real connection with one another, as in Plato and Descartes, but are united to one another essentially since the soul is the *form* of the body. The soul is the form of a living thing first of all because it is what makes it a living body. The human, or rational, soul is the form of man since it is what makes him specifically different from the other animals. It is form which gives a thing its specific difference from other things. A man is an animal but rational nature is specific to him and differentiates him from all other animals. However, making the soul the form of the body presents problems for the immorality of the soul, since how can the soul exist separately without a body when it is by nature the form of a body? This is a difficulty for which Aristotle never provided an answer, since he seems to have thought that the intellectual soul comes 'from without'[5] and is something divine, which thus reverts to the one great soul. There are two ways out of this dilemma: one is to say that the soul does not remain individual when it has no body to individuate it but souls become one universal soul. The other is to say that the soul remains individual because it returns to successive bodies by re-incarnation. St Thomas, however, says that the separated soul can continue in existence because it is a *subsistent* form, that is a form which has existence in itself. In this he was going beyond Aristotle, for whom the intellectual soul is the form but not a subsistent form. By a subsistent form St Thomas means that the

---

[4] *Quodlibet* II 1, 1; IV 5, 8
[5] *De Generatione Animalium* II c. 3 736b29.

soul exists in the body but not as though it depends on the body for its existence.

For St Thomas a form either has existence of itself or is that by which something composite exists. A thing ceases to exist when it loses its form: some matter ceases to be wood when it loses the form of wood and assumes the form of ash. The human soul is a form which has existence of itself because it has an activity of its own which is not the exercise of a corporeal part.[6] A thing can only subsist, that is exist in its own right, if it has an activity of its own, which the intellectual soul has, namely thinking, since this is not the power or function of any organ of the body. How is it then that we require a brain for thinking? St Thomas replies that the brain is not needed for the *exercise* of thinking but for the *object* of thinking, since we cannot think of things without turning to images, for having which we do need the brain.[7]

But if the intellectual soul's own activity is not the exercise of an organ of the body, how is it united to the body as its form? On the one hand, it is not a subsistent form unless it has an activity of its own; on the other hand, if this activity is independent of the body, it seems that it is not united to the body. The solution provided by St Thomas is that the intellect is a *power* of the soul which is the form of the body. The advantage of this is that St Thomas, in keeping with today's preferred way of speaking, can show that it is not merely a mind but a *man* who thinks, just as we do not say a man's eyes see but *he* sees. One might say that we do not have souls but just minds and that that this is enough to explain how we are something material which can think, but if we only have a mind and not also a soul one has not explained what thinking is a power *of*, unless you make it the power of the body, which it does not seem to be. One explanation avoiding the soul is to say that the mind is a 'capacity' of the body. This leaves us asking how is the mind a capacity of the body when thinking is not the power of a bodily organ? It also fails to account for what gives the body its unity, which is its form. St Thomas, however, by making the

[6] *Quaestiones de Anima* q. 14.
[7] *Summa* I 75, 2 ad 3.

intellect a power of the soul can show that though thinking is not a function of a body yet it is a man who thinks because that whereby he thinks is united to the whole of him as his form.

St Thomas argues that the human soul is immortal and incorruptible because it is immaterial, and hence indivisible. Immaterial things do not have parts, though they do have *powers*. The human soul is immaterial because it can know the natures of all kinds of bodies, which the senses cannot, so it cannot itself have the nature of a body, just as you cannot see all colours through a medium which has some colour or through tinted glass. When Aquinas claims that the soul is immaterial because we can think of the natures of kinds of things apart from the matter of individual things, which is to think of them immaterially, he is only saying much the same thing as a modern philosopher, Frege (1848-1925), has done: when I consider the separate items of a set of things and disregard the characteristics which distinguish them, I get a general concept under which they fall.[8] When I disregard the characteristics which distinguish Burmese from Siamese cats, I am left with the concept of cat. If the soul were not immaterial, it would only know things as the senses do, which is as individuals and not generally. However, the intellect still does not seem to differ from the senses, since the objects of sight are not materially in the eye either, as there is no lump of gold in the eyes when it is seeing gold. But colours still have the same mode of existence in the power of sight as they do in things, which is in matter; but this is not so in the mind. The human soul can exist on its own because in its way of knowing things it is rather raised above the body and is not dependent on it. Thus it is not comprehended by the body. Although it is the form of the body, it is not comprehended by it since it exceeds the capacity of the body in the way it knows things. But the sensitive souls of animals perish with their bodies since they are limited to the senses and so have no activity apart from the activity of a part of the body. The human soul can survive because it has an activity of its own.

[8] *The Foundations of Arithmetic* 34.

Another argument which St Thomas puts forward for the immortality of the soul is that something no longer exists when it loses its form but a form cannot lose itself, so what is in itself a subsistent form cannot be destroyed.[9] Strictly speaking, when a material thing ceases to exist, neither matter nor form corrupts but the composite whole does. When we die, the body defects from the existence which it had in common with the soul.[10]

St Thomas neither accepts that we are absorbed into one soul, which would destroy our individuality, nor reincarnation, since the soul is the form of the body and hence can be the form of only *one* body. Separated souls do not lose their individuality because they are related to different bodies, one soul to one body.[11] Numerically the same body is raised up since even in this life the identity of a body is not material identity, for the old man is the same individual as the child he once was, though all the matter of his body has been entirely changed and renewed several times over. Numerically the same man remains because new matter receives the same form. The separated soul remains in its existence, as it has existence of itself, with the same existence as it had in this life, which was the existence of the whole, since the body only gets its existence from the soul, by which it is something living. An identical person is raised up because the body is restored to the same *personal* existence as it had previously in this life. As Aquinas points out, the resurrection is not like melting down a bronze statue and remaking a replica of it out of the same bronze, which he says would not be numerically the same stature but two statues with two distinct forms, for the body that is restored is numerically the same body because there is the same form, the soul having persisted in its existence.[13]

On the question of how we know the soul, St Thomas departed from St Augustine, who thought we can know the

[9] *Summa* I 75, 6 ad 3.
[10] *QQ de Anima* 1. 1 ad 14.
[11] *Contra Gentiles* II c. 81.
[12] *Quodlibet.* VIII q. 3, 5.
[13] *Ibid.* XI q. 6, 6 ad 3.

essence of the soul, which would be like being able to see the soul,[14] and said that we only know it as we know other things, which is as they are actual. Hence we only know the mind in its actions of thinking, judging, willing, deciding etc.[15] Only knowing powers which are subsistent in themselves can know themselves since self-reflection is an immanent activity, that is one which remains within itself. By self-reflection the mind can reflect on its own activity. The reason why the senses do not know themselves is because they are not subsistent in themselves but are powers of bodily organs.[16] The eye does not see itself, nor a mirror reflect itself, except when it reflects a mirror opposite to it, which has a reflection of the first mirror in it. But this is not reflecting *on* itself, which is what the mind can do.

A prominent part of St Thomas' account of the soul is the distinction between the passive and active intellect, which he took over from Aristotle, who said that the intellect can become all things and produce all things. The intellect is passive because it starts as a *tabula rasa* which is capable of acquiring the concepts of all kinds of things from buttons to clouds. St Thomas' word for it is the 'possible' intellect. The intellect is passive because it is potential *for* something, for having intelligible likenesses. And it is active because it makes its concepts of sensible things; it does not get them from outside but forms them itself. The active intellect is the power for getting likenesses from individual things; the passive intellect is the power for receiving these likenesses. However, they are not two intellects; rather they are one and the same intellect which is active and passive. This is not clear in Aristotle since he thought that the passive intellect perishes and the active intellect returns to a universal intellect, 'being something divine', as he says.[17] Aquinas defends the unity of our intellect; neither the active nor passive intellect in us is a part of another intellect outside. His point is that the active intellect is a power of the individual soul, not a separate intellect in which everyone shares.

[14]*De Trinitate* X 10.
[15]*Summa* I 87, 1.
[16]*Ibid.* I 14, 2 ad 1.
[17]*De Anima* III c. 5 430a25.

We cannot think of things without turning to impressions (*phantasmata*, literally appearances). This is because what a horse is only actually exists in individual horses, which we apprehend by sense and imagination. We turn to impressions and images when we use images and examples to illustrate (from *illustrare*, to light up) what we are trying to explain to others or to understand ourselves. Thus the Danish physicist, Bohr, at the suggestion of Rutherford, thought of electrons orbiting round a nucleus as moons revolve round Jupiter when he was trying to discover the inner structure of the atom. We write down letters and signs when doing algebra, so that we can see the problem more clearly. We also need to turn to impressions and images, because the further things are from the source of light, which is one and simple in its source, the more they are diversified and refracted. If we only had the simpler and more general ideas with which angels see things, we would not know them more clearly, as they do, but less distinctly and more confusedly.

The forms of material things are not in themselves intelligible for us but have to be got out of, or abstracted from, matter. This is because material things can make impressions on the senses since the seeing power, for instance, exists in the same way as they do, which is in matter, but they cannot impress a likeness on anything immaterial, such as the intellect is. Thus some active power of the mind is needed to get its likenesses from the likenesses of things, which are in the senses. The light of the mind has to be directed on to sense-impressions to make them actually intelligible. The active intellect is like a light.[18] To abstract intelligible likenesses from the impressions of things is to consider what belongs to the idea of a kind of thing, of what belongs to the nature of a duck as distinct from a wader, for example. That things have natures may require some explanation nowadays. However, we know that an ox is not a bison. And the reason why things are not scallops is because they do not have the nature of scallops. The senses do not *do* anything with the impressions they receive from outside things; they are passive to them and only register things.

[18] *Summa* I 79, 3 ad 2.

St Thomas' account of how we make our concepts is quite
different from Augustine's theory of divine illumination. In
Thomas it is not the mind which is lit-up from outside but
sense-impressions which are lit-up by the mind.[19] In his view
God has given the mind sufficient light for knowing natural
things: 'he is the light who enlightens everyone coming into
the world' (*John* 1, 9). It is not by divine illumination that we get
the concepts of rhomboids and rodents.

There is a likeness in the sense in sensation and a likeness in
the mind when we think of something, which St Thomas calls
an 'intelligible likeness' (*species*). In Latin *species* means both
kind and appearance, just as we tell what *kind* a thing is from
its appearances. In Aquinas, *intelligere* does not just mean to
understand but very often to think of. Central to his thought
about the mind is that something is actualized by a form; so the
mind is actualized by having the form of things in thinking of
them. The intellect is informed by the form of what it thinks of;
a likeness of the thing being thought of is the form of the
intellect thinking of it. The form of the intellect is not a mental
image but an intelligible likeness. From the many impressions
of duck which I have seen, of eider duck, shell duck and so on,
I have formed the concept of duck; I have many impressions of
duck but one concept of duck.

St Thomas maintains that we know things, not just our ideas
of them. It is as thought he had an answer four hundred years
in advance for Locke (1632-1704), who thought that we do not
know things themselves but our ideas of them: 'the mind in all
its thought and reasoning hath no immediate objects but its
own ideas'.[20] Ideas for Locke included sense-impressions. For
St Thomas ideas, or likenesses, are not *what* we know but that
by which we know things.[21] He draws an analogy with sense: what
we see is not the image in the eye but the thing of which there
is an image in the eye. The image in the eye is that by which I
see something, for I do not look at images but at things; I do not
look at an image of a tree but at the tree. 'A stone is not in the

---

[19] *Ibid.* i 85, 1 ad 4.
[20] *An Essay concerning Human Understanding* Bk III c. 1.
[21] *Summa* I 85, 2.

mind but a likeness of stone. Yet it is a stone that is thought of, not a likeness of stone, except when the mind is reflecting on itself.'[22] Ideas are only what we know, rather than that by which we know things, when the mind reflects on its own thinking and concepts of things. Although we know things, nonetheless St Thomas says that our words do not signify things directly but the mind's conceptions, and things by means of the mind's conceptions of them.[23] For Aquinas 'lion' expresses the lion nature since it signifies the definition of a lion. When you look up 'lion' in the dictionary, what you get is a definition of lion. To use Russell's terms, 'lion' is a concept but *denotes* individual lions.

St Thomas holds that we can know things in their actual existence: 'The eye does not know a stone by the existence it has in the eye, but by a likeness of a stone which is in the eye it knows a stone in the existence it has outside the eye'.[24] This is much more satisfactory than the scepticism of Hume (1711-1776) who said that we do not know things as they really are but only as they affect the senses, since he held that the only existences we are aware of are our perceptions. For Russell physics is not the study of things themselves but of sense-data, since sense-data are all we know of the external world. Although one might expect empirical philosophy, that all there is is what we know by sense and experience, to be particularly suited to the natural sciences, which are founded on the empirical method of observation and experiment, Aquinas provides a more useful philosophy for natural science since he maintains that we can know objects as they are in reality outside of ourselves.

Things can exist in two ways, which St Thomas calls their *natural* and *intentional* existence.[25] The natural existence of something is how it exists in itself, which is materially for material things. Its intentional existence is how it exists in thought. There is no piece of quartz in the mind thinking of quartz. This may seem a curious use of 'intentional' for us

---

[22] *Ibid.* I 14, 6 ad 1.
[23] *De Interpretatione* I lect. 2, 5.
[24] *Summa* I 76, 2 ad 4.
[25] *Ibid.* I 56, 2 ad 3.

today, since intention usually has the practical sense of going to do something, but the two senses are not unrelated since our intention in doing something is our object in doing it, and 'intention' in the older, medieval sense is equivalent to an object of thought. As the object of doing something is called one's 'intention', so the object of thought has intentional existence in the mind. Intention comes from *intendere*, which meant to stretch a bow, and thus to aim at an object. The Koh-i-noor diamond, for instance, has its natural existence where it is kept in the Tower of London and intentional existence in the mind of anyone thinking of it.

Towards the end of his life, in 1269, St Thomas was recalled to Paris to stem the growing influence of ideas derived from Averroes. These were especially the doctrine that there is but one universal mind in which we all share. This of course had considerable consequences for Christian belief in the immortality of the individual soul and undermined the foundation of morality, based on reward and punishment, without which the whole edifice of morals would collapse, since if we all share one mind, how am I to know that it is really me and not someone else who is responsible for my actions, which deserve reward or blame? Nor is Averroism merely a curious idea of the past, since it can still be met today, even among natural scientists: for example, E. Schrödinger, whose question was: How does a single world view crystallize out of many minds? His answer was that there is a single consciousness, which he likened to a great canvas on which the memories and experiences of each person have their patch.[26] When someone with this sort of belief is asked to explain our individuality, they may reply that it lies in the different ways we respond to the universal mind. This seems to have been the reason why Avicenna (980-1037) also held the idea: we possess the same concepts because we get them from one mind. St Thomas' reply to Avicenna is that we do not have universal ideas because there is a universal mind but because the mind is immaterial and so can think of things generally.[27]

---

[26] *What is Life? Mind and Matter* p. 145.
[27] *QQ de Anima* q. 2 ad 6.

Averroes (1126-1198) held this belief because he thought it to be the correct interpretation of Aristotle when he says that the intellect is 'separate'. Averroes may have been right about what Aristotle himself thought, but Aquinas' reply to him is that the intellect is not separate in its existence but in its *activity*, in that it does not involve a corporeal organ.[28] Aquinas contends that Averroes' doctrine is as much against reason as it is against Christian faith. It is clear from Aquinas' refutation of him that he was not simply concerned to defend Christian belief in immortality but above all to show that thinking is the action of this and that person; that our thinking is something *we* do ourselves. If we all shared in a universal intellect, thinking would not really be something which *I* do but which someone else does through me; thinking would be *occurring* in me but it would not be my action, which could properly be attributed to me. Thinking is not the action of this and that person unless their intellect is their own. Thinking is not my action unless the principle of thinking is a power of *my* soul and not of some external mind.

Averroes' way of explaining the union of the universal mind with anyone was to say that its idea also resides in the impressions of that person, as we think of things by turning to impressions. But Aquinas' comment on this is that if that is the way we show that it is we who think, it is like saying that a wall sees, rather than is seen, when someone's sight is joined with the appearances of colour in it.[29] Since, however, a wall does not see but is seen, Averroes fails to show that thinking is the action of this and that person; rather it is done by an outside mind. Thomas points out that Averroes' idea is also contrary to experience since everyone experiences that it is him or herself who thinks. Thomas also remarks that if there were only one mind, 'all political discussion would come to an end',[30] as we see in totalitarian states, in which only the mind of the one party is allowed. The intellect is not a separate mind but a

---

[28] *In De Anima* III lect. 8 no. 690.
[29] *De Unitate Intellectus* 66.
[30] *Contra Gentiles* II c. 76.

power of the soul and it is this which makes thinking the activity of this and that individual person.

St Thomas says that there are as many intellects as there are people; each person has his or her own mind. He distinguishes between a power and its exercise. That everyone shares a power does not mean that the power is numerically one in everyone but only that it comes from one source. But the exercise of the power is distinct in each person. There must be a superior power from which we get the power to think, which some held to be the universal mind. If we were to speak of there being one mind, St Thomas says, who was always ready to see what was right in the views of his opponents, it is God, from whom the power of every intellect is derived. There is a mark of the divine light in the human mind: 'the intellectual light in us is nothing other than a participated likeness of the uncreated light'.[31] But the soul is not made blessed in a separate intellect but in its Creator.

---

[31] *Summa* I 84, 5.

8

Christ

When St Thomas comes to discuss the Incarnation he draws
together, so to speak, the threads of theology, which is about
God and other things as they are the means by which man
comes to God, since divine and human nature are united in
Christ. All things come from God as their source and lead back
to him as their end, or goal. Thus the one who is God and man,
as man is our way of returning to God; we are led back, literally
'reduced', by his humanity to the end for which we have been
made, that is to everlasting beatitude, which lies in the vision
of God.[1] The things which God did as man make the path by
which we are saved. Thus the consideration of Christ falls into
two parts: how divine and human nature are united in him, or
how one and the same person is God and man, and his saving
work, which includes the mysteries of Christ's life. St Thomas
was able to bring fresh insights to the doctrine about Christ in
the West, since he was one of the first in the West to make use
of the acts of the early Councils of the Church, which were in
Greek because they had taken place in the Eastern half of the
Church and had only recently become available in the West.

One of the guiding principles of the Incarnation for St
Thomas is that the Son of God assumed flesh for the sake of our
salvation. St Thomas thought it fitting that God united human
nature to himself, so that he could raise up our hope and show
that it is possible for us to attain the end of human life, though
it is above our natural power. The Incarnation raises our hope

---

[1] *Summa* III 9, 2.

of coming to the blessed life with God when we see that the
distance between God and man has been bridged in Christ and
thus that it is possible to have the vision of God, in which the
mind is united with God.[2]

I

The first thing to be said about the Incarnation is that it is a
union. A union is the joining of two things in one. The key terms
here are person and nature. Person answers the question
'Who?' and is the subject of predications. Nature determines
the way something can act. The person has the existence;
nature says how a thing exists. Turtles cannot fly because they
do not have the winged nature of birds; flying is not anything
within the scope of their nature. Thomas explains that the
union in Christ is neither essential, fusing the two natures into
one, as Eutyches did, nor accidental but personal, that is in one
person. Eutyches, who was condemned at the Council of
Chalcedon in 451, did not see how Christ could be one unless
he only had one nature; so he confused the natures. Nestorius,
who was condemned at the previous Council of Ephesus in
431, took the opposite course of dividing Christ into two
persons since he did not see how Christ could have a true
human nature unless it were a human person; so he made him
into two persons. Thus Nestorius said that only a man was born
of Mary, and thus that Mary was not the Mother of God, since
the man Jesus for him was another person than the Son of God.
However, as St Thomas remarked, if the two natures are not
united in the same person they are not really united at all. St
Thomas' explanation of the Incarnation, in effect, follows that
of St Leo the Great in his letter to Flavian, which was adopted
at the Council of Chalcedon. Christ has two operations, divine
and human, as he has two natures: he does some things as God
and some as man. Majesty took humility; the former works
miracles, the latter suffers. Either nature acts in harmony with
the other. This doctrine is known as the *communicatio idiomatum*

[2]*Contra Gentiles* IV c. 54.

(a communication of the properties of either nature), for the properties of either nature are predicated of the same subject, or person.[3] The *communicatio idiomatum* enables us to say 'God was born', 'God suffered', 'God was crucified', since the person who was born, suffered and was crucified as man was also God. There is a good statement of it in St Leo, Letter 28 to Flavian: 'either nature acts in its proper way in communion with the other' (*agit enim utraque forma cum alterius communione quod proprium est*). Thus Christ cures a leper with divine power by the contact of his human nature in touching him with his hand. There is unity of person but distinction of natures: the person is not divided, the natures are not confused.

Human and divine nature are united in a unique way in Christ, since it is not by will, as with the blessed in the activity of knowing and loving God, which is by grace, but by personal existence, that is human nature in Christ has the existence of the person of the Son of God. Only in Christ has human nature been raised up to the union of personal existence, for however united the saints are with God they are not one person with him. Grace is not the means of the union in Christ, as Nestorius held, saying that the Word dwelt in Christ as God does in his saints, for grace flows *from* the union. Christ did not become the Son of God by divine favour because he was an exceptionally good man, which is a common view today, but he was the Son of God who became man. Nestorius also likened the union in Christ to the indwelling of the Word in him to God dwelling in his temple. If this were the right view, then, as St Thomas points out, Christ would not have said 'I am the light of the world' but 'The light of the world dwells in me'.[4] It also follows that, if the natures are not united in the same person but Christ is two persons, he has two existences, since a person is the subject of existence.

One of St Thomas' cardinal points about the Incarnation is that Christ has a single existence because he is one person. If he had a double existence, he would be two beings. He only has

[3] *Quaestio de Unione Verbi Incarnati* art. 5 ad 9.
[4] *In Ioannem* c. VIII lect. 2.

one existence, which is the existence of the eternal person who became man, because his human nature never existed on its own but only in union with the divine Word. His human nature did not exist before the Incarnation when the Son of God became man. If it had, it would have been a person in its own right, and the Son of God would have united a human person to himself. But he did not acquire a new personal existence when he became man; rather the same person subsisted in human as well as in divine nature, as his human nature only had the existence of an already existent person. God did not assume a man (*non assumpsit hominem*) but became man by assuming human nature. His human nature never existed as a person apart from the person of the Son of God. As St Thomas expresses it: Christ's human nature never existed by itself (*per se*) but only *in another* 'by an ineffable assumption'.[5]

For this reason Christ's human nature can be called an individual but not a person or supposit. The person who has the human nature is the eternal Son of God. Christ assumed an individual human nature but he was not another individual than the Son of God; he has an individual human nature but Christ is not several individuals.[6] His human nature is an individual human nature but not an individual existing by itself. Thus there are several individual things in Christ, Thomas says, but he is not several individuals because he assumed human nature in an individual but this individual is not another individual than the Son of God. Christ is one person because his human nature is drawn into communion with the complete existence of the divine person who assumed it, as the body will be drawn into the soul's existence at the resurrection, though not as body and soul constitute one nature, for Christ has two natures, but as they constitute one person.[7] However difficult we may find it that Christ's real human nature is not a person by itself, if it were an independent person, Christ would be two persons, as Nestorius held, since if he is not one person Christ is not God.

[5] *Q. de Unione Verbi Incarnati* art. 2.
[6] *Quodlibet* III 2, 5 (Easter 1270); IX 2, 2 (Advent 1257).
[7] *Summa* III 2, 6 ad 2.

The touchstone for St Thomas of how we are to talk about Christ is the way Scripture speaks about him. How, for instance, can it say that the one by whom all things exist has been perfected by suffering (*Hebrews* 2, 10)? For the one by whom all things exist is God but God does not suffer; a man is perfected by suffering. Or how can St Paul say that the Lord of glory has been crucified (*1 Corinthians* 2, 8), for the Lord of glory is God but a man was crucified? At the foundation of St Thomas' discussion is a simple piece of grammar: that we predicate things of a subject. For us to be able to predicate divine things of a man and human things of God, as Scripture does, there must be the same subject, or person, who is both God and man. Only a union of the natures in one person allows us to do this; Nestorius rendered impossible the attribution of human and divine things to the same person since Christ was two persons for him. Since he made Christ into two persons he could not say that God was crucified or died or was buried, which we do because the person (subject) who was crucified had divine as well as human nature. We can say that God died because the man who hung on the cross was personally the Son of God and not another person. God suffered but divine nature did not suffer; he did not suffer in his divine nature but *as* man. For we distinguish between that *about which* we speak, which is about a subject, and that *according to which* we say something about it, which in the case of Christ is in some respect, as he is God or as he is man.[8] When we ask *about whom* we are speaking, Christ is one and the same person; when we ask how or *according to what* we say something of him, he is one and another, human and divine. Thus the man called Jesus does divine things, such as calm a storm at sea and restore sight to the blind, and the Son of God is tired, thirsty and hungry.

We can say both 'God is man' and 'Man is God' since there is one and the same subject of divine and human nature in Christ; that is there is the one person who has divine and human nature. 'God is man' does not mean that divine nature is human, which would be to predicate human of divine

[8] *Ibid.* III 16, 4.

nature, but that someone with divine nature also has human nature. 'Man' means having humanity or an individual subsisting in human nature. We can say 'Man is God' because 'man' stands for any supposit of human nature: 'man' signifies human nature but *stands for* a person. But 'God' can either mean the person or the nature, since God is identical with his nature. God stands for person in 'God from God' (the Son from the Father) but means the nature in 'Man is God', since it predicates divine nature of someone with human nature. We can call anything 'God' which has divine nature and anything 'man' which has human nature.

Although 'God is man' and 'Man is God' are reversible statements and both are permissible, the same does not hold of 'God became man' and 'Man became God', since only the first of these is allowed. Similarly, 'Christ began to be man' is only true if by Christ we mean the divine person, who is not called Christ until the Incarnation, but not true if it implies that Christ began to exist, since the person who is called Christ has no beginning of existence but is the eternal Son. All that St Thomas says about the Incarnation is secured by the one verse: 'The Word was made flesh' (*John* 1, 14), which excludes all misunderstandings about Christ since the Word is the subject who became flesh; not that God was changed by becoming flesh but the Word became flesh when he became man by taking human nature.

For St Thomas the Incarnation is not the ascent of a man, as in modern views, but the *descent* of the Word.[9] A man did not become God, which is an ancient heresy known as 'adoptionism', but a divine person became man. There is one person because it was this person who became man, 'was made flesh'. 'No one has ascended into heaven except he who came down from heaven, the Son of man, who is in heaven' (*John* 3, 13). It was not a man who came down from heaven, since Christ did not come into the world like some extra-terrestrial being from outer space but was born of a woman, Mary. It was then a divine person who came down from heaven and this person is also man, the Son of man. It was the same person who said

9 *Ibid.* III 33, 3 ad 3.

'I came down from heaven' and 'I ascend to my Father' (*John* 6, 38; 20, 17). There was descent before there could be exaltation; there is no descent but only exaltation if Christ was a man who became the Son of God. The descent was his emptying but this emptying was not putting off the divine nature which he already possessed but his assuming the form of a servant, that is human nature.[10] The emptying is not the putting off of divine nature since Jesus says that he who came down from heaven still is in heaven. Jesus was not a mere man who deserved to be raised up to divine status, which would make him Son of God by grace and divine favour; rather it is the other way round: a man did not become God but God became man. A man is not deified, as in contemporary ideas about Christ, but God is 'humanized' (*humanatum*), to use St Thomas' expression.[11]

God became man does not mean that the whole Trinity is incarnate but that God is man in one person, since human nature can only be united to one person in union of person. God did not assume humanity in general but an individual human nature. It is appropriate that the second person of the Trinity became man, so that man who is created in the image of God is recreated by the person who is the Image of God. It is also fitting that the person who is called the Wisdom of God became man since man has been made to know the truth, especially the First Truth, by which he advances in wisdom. It was for this purpose that 'the divine wisdom was clothed in flesh, so that he might come into the world to manifest the truth'.[12]

St Thomas says that there have been two basic errors about Christ: one, that he was a mere man; the other, that he was not really a man at all but his human aspect was only an appearance, and is hence known as 'docetism' from the Greek word for to seem, *dokein*. His concern to uphold the integrity of Christ's human nature may explain the frequent times he makes a special point of refuting Appolinarius (d. 390), whom we

[10]*In Philippos* c. 2 lect. 2.
[11]*Summa* III 16, 3 ad 2.
[12]*Contra Gentiles* I c. 1.

hardly mention today. Apollinarius denied that Christ has a human soul, since he conceived of the union of divine and human nature in Christ as that of the soul and body, so that the Word takes the place of the soul in Christ. He thought that the Word is united to flesh as the soul is to the body. If this were a right view of the Incarnation, Christ did not have a rational nature like ours, as he would lack a human soul. However, that the Word 'became flesh' does not mean that he was only joined to flesh but that he truly became man. Apollinarius was taking 'flesh' in a narrow sense, not in the sense of became man, as flesh stands here for human nature. St Thomas argues against Apollinarius from the evidence of Scripture, which speaks of Christ's soul and ascribes to him human emotions: 'My soul is sorrowful to the point of death' (*Matthew* 26, 38). Sadness was not a reaction of his body but of his soul. Christ's human nature was not a mere puppet of God but was animated by a human soul with free will. Thomas notes that when Christ prayed, 'Not as my will but thy will be done', there was some conflict of wills here but 'my will' cannot be his divine will since this is one with the Father's will; so 'my will' must refer to his human will, which is contrasted with the Father's will.

II

Our belief about *who* Christ is is important for our estimation of what he *did* for us. If he was a mere man, then we have not been saved by God and we do not have a divine Saviour, but Christ's death on the cross was the offering of a man, which was accepted by God. The significance of his passion and death derive from the person (*who* he is) who suffered, who was none other than the Son of God. The life he gave up has the value that it does because it is united to the godhead in him. St Thomas balances the theory of the redemption, as it stood in the West, which might appear to make it mostly a matter of justice and of satisfying for sin, by bringing out more fully how it was wrought by love. The Western theory of redemption, as we find it in St Anselm (1033-1109) was, very briefly, this: justice requires that satisfaction be made for sin; but since the offence was against God, the satisfaction required for it was beyond anything which man could make by himself; yet for satisfaction to be made, it needed to be man who made it since he had committed the offence; thus it required someone who was both man but more than man — the God-man. Christ satisfies for sin by paying the penalty of sin, which is death. However, it is not true that Anselm makes redemption solely a matter of justice without including any mention of love, since he says that though Christ died in obedience to the Father's command, he died freely (*sponte*) as he willed the will of his Father.[13] Christ's death does not merely save us because it meets the requirements of justice but because of the greatness of the love with which he died, which St Thomas says was 'more than enough'. St Thomas' point is well expressed by a word coined by the English poet, Richard Crashaw, in his poem *Caritas nimia*: Christ has 'overbought' us. Christ's death is a sacrifice because he died freely out of love.[14] Christ offered himself; others did not offer him — they merely slew him.

St Thomas says that Christ's death is a sacrifice, because it is a peace offering, by which he reconciles us with God. When St Paul says that Christ was made 'sin' for our sake (*II Corinthians* 5, 21), he does not mean that Christ was sinful in any way but that he was made a sacrifice for sin, as it was laid down in the Old Testament that sacrifice was to be made for sin. The background of St Thomas' thinking here is to be found in the three kinds of sacrifice spoken of in the Old Testament, especially in *Leviticus* chapters 3 and 16. These are the peace offering, the sin offering or expiation, and the holocaust. St Thomas remarks that only one who is himself without sin can be a sin offering for sinful humanity, otherwise he would be one of sinful men for whom sacrifice needed to be made. He notes further that St Paul says that God was reconciling us to himself in Christ; in Christ, because he reconciled us in one who is also man, since what needed to be taken away was in man.[15]

---

[13]*Cur Deus Homo* I c. 9.
[14]*Summa* III 47, 2 ad 3.
[15]*In II Corinthos* c. V lect. 5.

It was not absolutely necessary for God to die to save us; he could have saved us in some other way and wiped out sin by a mere word. But without Christ's death we would not have an example of dying to sin ourselves. The benefits of Christ's passion for us are, first, liberation from sin, since by giving up his life he paid the price of redemption, just as slaves are liberated from slavery by the payment of a ransom. Thus Christ's death redeems us from the slavery of sin. Secondly, we see how much God loves us. And, thirdly, this provokes us to love God in response to his love. Christ's death is our liberation, and generally the usefulness of the Incarnation, St Thomas says, is our liberation. His death is our liberation from sin and his resurrection is our liberation from death. Our liberation will only be complete at our resurrection when we will finally be freed from the necessity of dying, which came in through sin.[16] Our liberation from sin by his passion works in us by means of the sacraments, and our liberation from death by his resurrection will be effective at the resurrection of the dead.

The things which Christ did in his humanity are saving for us through the divinity, to which it is united. St Thomas sees in the mysteries of Christ's life a sacramental significance, in that what he did in his life is to be repeated in us. Their end is to lead us to the life of glory, which Christ as man entered by his resurrection. On the baptism of Christ, St Thomas says that he was baptized to provide us with an example that would bring others to baptism and to show that baptism was the way men would enter heaven. The elements of the event reveal the effects of baptism. The opening of the heavens shows us that by baptism the sin which blocks entry into heaven is taken away and that the way to heaven, which had been closed by Adam's sin, is once again open. Although the heavens were opened at Christ's baptism, no one could enter heaven before his passion, since his passion is the cause of the opening of heaven as it took away the sin which closed it; but the heavens were opened at Christ's baptism to show us that the effect of his passion is applied to individuals by baptism. The Holy Spirit descends on Christ when he is baptized to show that through baptism we

---

[16]*QQ. de Anima* q. 1 ad 5.

receive the Holy Spirit. Thus the complete Trinity is revealed in Christ's baptism: the Father in the voice declaring, 'This is my beloved Son'; the Son is the one standing in the water; and the Holy Spirit in the dove, the symbol of peace through sin being taken away. As Christ is manifested as the Son of God at his baptism, so we can know that by baptism we become adopted sons of God, sharing in his Sonship.

The Trinity is also revealed at the Transfiguration of Christ: the Father again in the voice which speaks from heaven, the Son shining in glory on the mountain and the Holy Spirit this time in the bright cloud. As baptism is the sign of our first regeneration, so St Thomas calls the Transfiguration the 'sacrament' of our second regeneration, which will be of the body at the resurrection of the dead.[17] Christ is transfigured straight after his first prediction that he would suffer, and rise again, to show the Apostles that his passion leads to glory. His transfiguration is a sign that we will also be configured with Christ in the glory of his resurrection, which is here foreshadowed as the glory of his soul flowed into his body. But at the Transfiguration this glory was only transitory, not permanent, since his body had not yet entered immortal life. The light which lit up Christ at his transfiguration was not a reflection of an external light but came from within him. The brightness of his garments, St Thomas adds, represents the brightness (*claritas*) of the saints who 'will shine like the sun in the kingdom of their Father' (*Matthew* 13, 43). St Thomas quotes from St John Chrysostom, observing that the appearance of Moses and Elijah on either side of Christ shows us that Jesus was not Elijah or any of the prophets, as some said he was, and thus implies that he is the Christ.

Between Christ's passion and resurrection came his descent to the lower regions, or Sheol, which shows us that his salvation not only affects those who live after him but also includes those who lived under the Old Testament. Christ descended to the place where the just were detained until the gates of heaven were opened, since they were excluded from heaven until Christ had redeemed them and himself entered the life of

[17]*Summa* III 45, 4 ad 2.

glory as man. If Christ descended to the damned in Hell, it was only to confute them by his presence. Christ's soul could descend to the lower regions because its union with the Word was not dissolved when it was separated from his body in death. Before he rose again his soul went to where the spirits of the just were and appeared to them in his soul. As the passion of Christ is our liberation, so he liberated the just who were waiting in Hades by his descent thither. St Thomas says that he liberated them by 'visiting and illuminating them'; 'he will give light to those who sit in darkness'.[18]

Since the passion by itself would not have been enough for salvation, which consists in the reintegration of the human person and of human nature, it also requires the resurrection of the body. Christ could only show that he has overcome death by dying, since he could not rise from the dead unless he first died. His resurrection raises our hope of rising from the dead, for it is the exemplar of our resurrection, when we will be configured with him on the pattern of his glorious body. Christ showed that he had risen by 'many signs' (*Acts* 1, 3) to manifest the truth of his resurrection and the glory of the risen person. He appeared to certain people after his resurrection to show that he had risen, but only intermittently, and not all the time, to let them know that he was now in another life, since he was no longer subject to death. He is 'the first-fruits of the dead' (*I Corinthians* 15, 20) since he was the first to rise again to immortal life, in which one no longer has to die. In this Christ's resurrection differed from that of Lazarus, who was raised from the dead to the same kind of life as before and who died again. The Apostles knew that Christ had truly risen since they recognized by his wounds that he had numerically the same body as was crucified.[19] Christ rose with a glorious body but it was still a body of the same nature, though it was now in a different state since it was a spiritual body, that is a body which is free since it is wholly subject to the spirit.[20] St Thomas enables us to understand how a risen body might still be a body of the

[18]*Ibid.* III 52, 4 ad 1.
[19]*Ibid.* III 55, 6 ad 4.
[20]*Ibid.* III 54, 1 ad 2.

same nature as ours with the help of an analogy: stained glass, which appears dull and opaque when it is not seen against light, is transformed in appearance when light shines through it, though it remains the same glass.[21]

The Ascension causes our salvation as it opens up the way to heaven, where Christ has gone as our High Priest to plead for us. The Father has pity on us when he sees the human nature which Christ took with him into heaven at his Ascension. The Ascension also causes our salvation by increasing faith, hope and charity. It raises faith by lifting up our minds to things unseen; it raises our hope of coming to where he has ascended; and our charity by directing our love to the things which are above. Likewise, St Thomas related the Passion and the Resurrection to the virtues of faith, hope and charity; they also cause our salvation by increasing these virtues, which are necessary for it. Thus he says that Christ rose to 'instruct' our faith. When Christ ascended, he 'led captivity captive' (*Ephesians* 4, 8) by taking with him into heaven the souls of the just who had been held captive in Sheol until he opened the way into heaven and delivered them from their captivity by his descent to the lower regions.

Christ assumed the consequences of sin, though he was without sin himself, in order to liberate us from sin. He assumed those infirmities of human nature which it was profitable for him to bear for our salvation, such as pain, weariness and hunger; but not ignorance, which St Thomas did not think would have been any help to us, since Christ came rather to show us the truth and it would have been contrary to his being said to be 'full of grace and truth' (*John* 1, 14). He assumed the weaknesses of human nature so that his humanity might be more manifest, which is our way to God.[22] The Incarnation was not truly the mercy of God unless he entered into our misery. But unless Christ possessed the knowledge which the blessed have in seeing God, he could not lead others to beatitude, which is what he came to do. To lead others to beatitude, Christ had the knowledge of it himself. Christ knew

[21]*Ibid.* III 54, 3 ad 1.
[22]*Ibid.* III 14, 1 ad 4.

that he was God, since the man who was seen to say 'Before Abraham was I am' (*John* 8, 58) was the same person as the Son of God. Christ is the Truth itself, which cannot deny itself. For St Thomas Christ's sinlessness is a matter of his truth, since to have sinned would have been for Christ to have denied himself.[23]

When writing about the grace of Christ, Thomas is but drawing out the meaning of St John's expression, 'full of grace and truth'. Grace was given to Christ *for us*. Grace flows from his divinity into his humanity, which is joined to it, and from his humanity into us, who are incorporated into his body. It is when talking about the grace of Christ that St Thomas brings in the Church, which is the body of Christ, and by being incorporated into which we receive the grace which flows into his humanity. The grace of Christ overflows (literally 'redounds', *redundat*) from the head into the body. Christ is the head of his body, the Church, as man since he shares the same nature as we have. Head and body comprise as though one 'mystical person', he says.[24] It is for this reason that by his passion Christ can merit for us, since we are made part of his body. As grace flows from his divinity into his humanity, so he is the source of grace for us, since he shares human nature with us. No sacraments gave grace before the Incarnation because grace comes through his humanity. Grace flows from Christ into his body like a life-giving transfusion into the members of his body (*influentia transfundetur*). Grace does not come to us by nature but by the 'personal action' of Christ; 'personal', because it is not by nature that we receive grace.[25] For we do not receive the benefits which his death won for us merely by having human nature, which derives from Adam, but by being incorporated into the body of Christ.[26]

[23] *In II Timotheum* c. 2 lect. 2.
[24] *Summa* III 48, 2 ad 1.
[25] *Ibid.* III 8, 5 ad 1.
[26] *Ibid.* III 19, 4 ad 3.

9

***

Signs and Realities

Sacraments belong to the chain of causes by which God communicates to us his life and power. Since we are not just spirit but body as well, our contact with God is not purely spiritual, or immediate, but God adapts the way he comes to us to our corporeal nature so that we receive grace through visible, audible and tangible means. The sacraments are first of all *signs*, but a special kind of sign: which sanctify us. We have signs of the interior action of God in us, since our knowledge begins with the senses: as we need to turn to impressions to think of things, so we have visible signs to make the things of faith more vivid to us. The sacraments signify more expressively (*expressior*) the grace of Christ.[1]

Though we may think of sacraments primarily as material symbols, St Thomas places the emphasis on the word: the words of a sacrament signify more than its symbol, he says, since the symbol only gets its meaning from the words. In their structure of word and symbol the sacraments are like Christ, who is the Word joined with sensible flesh as words are joined to sensible things in them.[2] Thus they are an extension of the Incarnation, the Word made flesh.

A sacrament causes, that is it brings about, the effect of grace which is intended by the words and represented by the action of the sacraments. They do not only signify but are also causes of the grace they signify since they bring about what they signify by their words. This does not mean that there are two causes of

[1] *Summa* III 60, 5 ad 3.
[2] *Ibid.* III 60, 6.

grace: God and the sacraments, but God remains the sole author of grace since Christ's humanity is only a source of grace as it is united to his divinity. The sacraments are instrumental causes just as Christ's humanity was instrumental in healing by divine power, as when he touched the leper. Instruments are powerless to produce their effect by themselves, for example a saw to cut, but they require an agent to be effective. The sacraments get their power to bring about interior effects in us from their author God, who uses them as means. As instruments, the sacraments may be called God's tools for reshaping our human nature in his image. Grace is caused instrumentally by the sacraments but principally by the Holy Spirit working in them. We have visible signs of grace because Christ gives us the Holy Spirit as God and man.[3] But he does not give us the Holy Spirit authoritatively (*auctoritative*), that is as the source, as man but only as his actions were saving through his divine power. We have sensible signs of his grace because he gives us it through his humanity. His humanity is instrumental in communicating the grace which comes principally, that is as from its source, from his divinity. The sacraments prolong Christ's actions of healing by word and touch, which he did as man. They cause grace because their author is Christ, who continues to act through his body, the Church, as he acted with divine power through his humanity when he healed the sick.

There were sacraments before Christ but they did no cause grace; they only signified it. These were the sacrifices and rites of the Old Testament, which were instituted to signify the passion of Christ and which pointed towards the sacrifice of Christ by prefiguring it, as did for the example the lamb sacrificed at the Passover. However, they did not give justifying grace but were signs of it, signifying the faith of those who lived before Christ's coming in him as the one to come. As we are only justified by faith in his passion, so people in the Old Testament were justified by faith in his passion as future. For we are not justified by the Old Law but by the mystery of the Incarnation.[4] If there had been sacraments which gave grace

---

[3] *In Titum* c. 3 lect. 1.

before Christ, there would have been no need for his death. The sacraments of the Old Law also differ from those of the New in that they did not share in a present reality but only prefigured something which was then still future. The sacraments derive their power from the cross: 'there is a power (*virtus*) in the cross'.[5] St Thomas calls Christ's death 'the sacrament of salvation', since by dying he gave an example of dying to sin.[6] Christ's death is recalled in baptism as we die with Christ, and in the Eucharist as it is a sacrifice, which is prefigured by the Passover lamb. We see that one of the chief criteria for what makes something a sacrament in St Thomas is that it applies the passion of Christ to us.

In St Thomas' view, all the sacraments justify because they all, in one way or another, represent the passion of Christ which takes away sin. We are justified by the sacraments because they apply to individuals the effects of Christ's passion, which justified us because it restored justice by paying the penalty for sin. Justification in St Thomas means, quite simply, the remission of sin. The justice which he is speaking of here is not legal justice but the justice which consists in the due order of the parts of human nature to one another and to God. It is not the virtue of justice we exercise in dealing with others but the right ordering of the interior disposition of our nature. Aristotle mentions this sort of justice when he asks whether someone can be unjust to themselves or only to another, and goes on to say that there is justice in a metaphorical sense between parts, whereby one is subordinate to another.[7] Since this order, of appetite to reason and of reason to God, was upset by the original sin, we are born in a state of injustice. Hence the putting right, or restoring, the loss of original justice is called 'justification'. As original justice was lost by sin, so taking away sin is justification. Sin is injustice because it is a disorder of the mind to God.

St Thomas brings it out that we are not solely justified by the

[4]*De Veritate* q. 28 art. 4.
[5]*Summa* III 62, 3.
[6]*Quodlibet* II 1, 2.
[7]*Ethics* V c. 11 1130b1.

death of Christ but by his resurrection as well, since justification is not merely removing something, namely sin, but has an end, which is new life. He was but making explicit a rather unnoticed point in St Paul: 'he was put to death for our sins and raised for our justification'.[8] Without the resurrection, Christ's passion would only have taken away sin, not restored us to new life. The resurrection justifies us as the end of the movement from sin to newness of life. His resurrection justifies us since through it we return to newness of justice, as Christ was raised by the Spirit who gives us new life.[9]

The chief sacrament is the Eucharist because it contains Christ himself, who is 'full of grace and truth'. The Eucharist differs from all the other sacraments in that it not only has a spiritual power but its material element is changed too, whereas water remains water in baptism, and oil in confirmation. The Eucharist has all those effects in our spiritual life which food does in our bodily life: it nourishes, restores strength, gives growth, delights and refreshes. It is the perfection of the spiritual life, St Thomas says. It is called the bread of angels because they feed on the Word by sight, as we talk about 'food for the mind', but we do not have sight but faith, as we are not united to Christ by plain vision but by faith now. Elsewhere, St Thomas says that we have sacraments because we walk by faith, not by sight, since the truth is seen in our present state as in an enigma.[10] The Eucharist is the sacrament of Christ's humanity, through which grace comes to us, but of his humanity in an invisible way, not as it is apprehended by sight but by faith.[11]

There are three possible ways that Christ could come to be present in the sacrament. First, he could enter it by local motion, as in moving from point A to B, but this is not how he is present because he is not present in it as in a place, locally, or on different altars as in different places. Secondly, he could come to be where bread and wine were by bread and wine being annihilated; but there is no annihilation of bread and

[8] *Romans* 4, 25.
[9] *Romans* 8, 11.
[10] *Summa* III 80, 2 ad 2.
[11] *Ibid.* III 75, 1.

wine since they do not become nothing but are changed into something — the Body and Blood of Christ. Thirdly, Christ could be present with bread and wine, alongside them, so that bread and wine remain, a theory known as 'consubstantiation'. If this were how he is present, he would not have said 'This is my body' but 'This bread is my body'.

Since bread and wine neither remain nor are they annihilated, there is a conversion of bread and wine into the body and blood of Christ. In every change something remains and something is altered. In a natural change there is the same subject of change. A natural change is a change of form; some matter which has one form assumes a new form, but this does not happen in the Eucharist since Christ does not become the form of bread. In the Eucharist it is the other way round: the appearances remain the same but there is a change of subject. Hence this change is called 'transubstantiation' since it is a change of substance, or of subject. There is no subject of this change since bread and wine do not have the passive power to become the body and blood of Christ. So they are changed into his body and blood by the active power of God. The change in the Eucharist is not a natural but supernatural one, wrought solely by the creative word of God.

This raises the question: How can the accidents, or sensible qualities, of bread and wine remain without a subject to inhere in, since they do not inhere in the body of Christ? They cannot naturally remain on their own without their subject, like the smile without the Cheshire cat. So St Thomas says that they are kept in existence by divine power with the same *existence* which they had previously in bread and wine. Accidents can continue to exist without their proper subject since effects depend more on the First Cause of all existence than on secondary causes.[12] Thus the place in the Creed, to which St Thomas assigns the Eucharist is mention of the almighty power of God.[13] It is because the appearances are not changed but remain the same that the sacrament retains its sign-value.

---

[12]*Ibid.* III 77, 1 ad 3.
[13]*Ibid.* II-II 2, 8 ad 6.

The change in the Eucharist is both like and unlike creation. It is like creation in that there is no subject of change, as creation itself was not a change of anything, and the words are instantaneous in their effect. But it is unlike creation in that it *is* a change, since something existent, namely bread and wine, is changed in it. At creation the words were imperative: 'Let their be light', but in the Eucharist they are in the indicative mood since they point to what they bring about. The words of consecration not only work effectively, as a creation, by bringing about something, but also sacramentally, that is by the power of their signification.[14] They bring about what they signify, namely that the body of Christ is present. The words work sacramentally, that is by the power of their signification. Consequently, their power to change follows their signification. The words effect nothing unless they signify, that is they do not effect anything if they do not mean what they signify, that this is the body of Christ.[15]

They signify what is effected. Thus 'This is my body' is demonstrative; they announce that something has become, not is becoming gradually, the body of Christ. The words say 'is' rather than 'becomes' because the change is instantaneous. So they only express the end of the change. St Thomas rather discountenanced saying that bread 'becomes' the body of Christ, except as 'becomes' is used in the phrase 'dawn becomes day', which means that after dawn comes day — first one thing, then another. But he allows '*from* bread (*ex pane*) is made the body of Christ'.[16]

The words of consecration not only affirm something but they bring about, or cause, what they affirm: they are *factiva* as well as *significativa*. They are related to the reality they bring about as God's creative word was to the things he called into existence. This is not just by the power of the Holy Spirit but by the instrumental power of the words themselves, which are spoken as though coming from the person of Christ himself.[17]

[14] *Ibid.* III 78, 2 ad 2.
[15] *In I Corinthos* c. 11 lect. 5.
[16] *Summa* III 78, 5 ad 1.
[17] *Ibid.* 78, 4 ad 1.

His words have the power to change, as they are the word by which all things were made. If God can create things out of nothing by his word, his words have the power to change what already exists into some new thing. The author of all being has the power to change what is of the being (*entitatis*) of one thing into the being of another thing.[18] The change in the Eucharist is effected by the power of God, which covers the being of everything. Since God's power extends to all things, he has the power to change not just the form of something but its whole being.

One source of the reluctance today to talk about 'transubstantiation' is a doubt about whether there is any such thing as substance. Another is that it is supposed that this explanation of the Eucharist is tied to a particular philosophy, Aristotle's. It is then worth seeing why Aristotle spoke about substance and that the Church was using this word some time before Aristotle was being used on any scale in theology. St Thomas was but taking up a word which had already been adopted by the Church to express her faith about the Eucharist long before anyone was being Aristotelian. The original use of the word 'substance' for the Eucharist was in contrast with 'figure'. In the profession of faith which was presented by Pope Gregory VII at the synod of Rome, in 1079, to Berenger, who held that the Eucharist was a mere figure, we find the expression, 'bread and wine are substantially converted'. The word 'transubstantiation' itself was first used by the Church at the Fourth Council of the Lateran, in 1215, some ten years before St Thomas was born: 'when bread has been transubstantiated into his body and wine into his blood'. Thus, when Aquinas uses 'substance' in his explanation of the Eucharist, he takes it from the usage of the Church, though he gives it an Aristotelian treatment. The Church, however, in using his explanation of the Eucharist at the Council of Trent, dissociated the doctrine of transubstantiation from Aristotelian philosophy by contrasting 'substance' not with 'accidents', as Aristotle does, but with '*species*', or appearances. St Thomas himself uses both

18*Ibid.* III 75, 4 ad 3.

'accidents' and 'species'; for the sake of simplicity, I will keep to 'appearances' from now on.

Aristotle speaks of substance because his question was: What makes some matter exist as flesh or bone, and some bricks and timber exist as a house, and says that this is their substance.[19] If there is no such thing as substance, there is nothing that a thing is essentially. But things are things as a whole. Is my image of a tree at which I am looking, for instance, an image of one thing, a tree, or merely of a lot of parts: leaves, branches etc.? If a thing is not anything as a whole, it is not one thing but a lot of things. But an animal or a plant is not just a heap of parts like a heap of leaves, nor even an assemblage of parts, as a machine is, since it has a unity. Aristotle comes to speak of substance from the basic principle of grammar, that we predicate things of a subject. We do not predicate qualities of one another but of their subject: white is not musical, but a white man may be musical. Man is the subject of white and musical. Aristotle's reason for speaking of substance is that a thing is not just its elements, since these continue to exist when it ceases to exist, so what it is is not itself one of its elements but something other than these, which we call its substance.

'This', St Thomas says, refers to substance, not to the appearances; it does not mean 'My body is signified by this'.[20] Substance answers the question, 'What is this?' Substance can be used to express the way Christ is present in the Eucharist, since substance is whole in the whole and whole in a part. The whole Christ is present in the Eucharist because of his resurrection, when his soul was reuinted with his body. Another analogy for Christ's presence in the sacrament is the way the soul is in the body: there is not a part of the soul in one part of the body and another part in another part but it is wholly in any part. For substance is not affected by the dimensions of a thing: Alice was as much a girl when she was tall as when she had shrunk. In the Eucharist there is a change of substance but not of the dimensions; Christ is present as substance is but not with

[19] *Metaphysics* VII c. 17 1041b11-1042a2.
[20] *Summa* III 78, 5 ad 1.

his own dimensions.[21] As he is wholly present in any part, Christ is wholly present in a fragment as well as in a whole host. He is not broken when the sacramental appearances are broken. In his hymn *Lauda Sion*, St Thomas says that there is a breaking of the sign but not of the reality. The senses are not wrong or deceived in seeing something being divided and multiplied when a host is broken. But since Christ's body itself is not divided or multiplied, it is the appearances which are broken. Thus St Thomas goes some way towards meeting Berengar, who had been worried about a too physical approach to the eating of the Eucharist, as though we bite Christ's flesh with our teeth in communion, with the quite straightforward principle that whatever is eaten is eaten in its own appearances. But since Christ is not present in this sacrament in his own but in sacramental appearances, so he is eaten in sacramental appearances. Christ's body is not broken when the sacramental appearances are, just as his body is not eaten in its own but in sacramental appearances.[22] Christ is *wholly* present beneath either *species* (appearances) of bread or of wine, since what is united in him in reality, as his body is in heaven, is not separated in the sacrament either.

Christ's body and blood are not signified by bread and wine but by the *appearances* of bread and wine. Bread and wine are not the signs but the appearances of bread and wine are. This point is overlooked by the modern theory of transignification, that bread and wine are the body and blood of Christ because that is the use they are designated for in the sacrament, just as silver becomes money when it is designated as coinage. But a silver coin is still silver, unlike bread and wine in the sacrament. Transignification is rather a nominal change, not a real one. Anyway, St Thomas pre-empts transignification as a way of explaining the Eucharist: Jesus, he says, 'insinuated the truth of this sacrament when he says 'is my flesh'. He does not say 'signifies my flesh' but 'is my flesh' because what is eaten in reality is truly the body of Christ'.[23]

---

[21] *Ibid*. III 76, 1 ad 3.
[22] *Ibid*. III 77, 7 ad 3.
[23] *In Ioannem* c. VI lect. 6.

It is an explicit part of St Thomas' view of the Eucharist that Christ is hidden beneath the outer appearances of the sacrament. When he was on earth, his humanity was seen but his divinity was hidden; here, however, his humanity is hidden too. As the priests used to enter the Holy of Holies through the veil, so we have to enter the humanity of Christ, which is presented to us under the veil of the appearances of this sacrament.[24] Christ's body in its own glorified state would be too bright for us to behold now by sight. We have to say that Christ's body is contained *beneath* the appearances of bread and wine because the appearances are not changed but only the substance which was contained beneath them. As the appearances are not changed, so neither are the dimensions. The Eucharist itself presupposes the resurrection since there could be no sacrament of his body unless it has been raised to life again. His body is in heaven in its own appearance, and dimensions, and present in the sacrament beneath sacramental appearances.[25] The body in the sacrament is identical with his natural body in heaven but it has a different *mode of existence* in heaven and in the sacrament: in heaven in its own appearance and in the sacrament as substance is. Christ's body can be in heaven and present in the sacrament at the same time because he has a *relation* to this sacrament.[26] The relation ceases when the sacramental appearances cease to exist; not that Christ depends on them to be really present but because the relation to the sacrament ceases when they disappear.

In the Eucharist we have the sacrament of the Truth, since Christ is present in it in truth. It really is his body, not merely a sign of it. It is also the sacrament of truth because there is no deception in it; the eyes are not deceived by what they see, which is the appearances of bread and wine, but faith apprehends the reality contained in the sacrament. Christ's humanity is apprehended here by faith, which rests on the words of Christ, who is the Truth and so does not lie. The

[24] *In Hebraeos* c. X lect. 2.
[25] *Summa* III 76, 5 ad 1.
[26] *Ibid.* III 76, 6.

Eucharist is also the sacrament of truth because the words used in it are the very words of Christ, who is the Truth himself:

Nil hoc verbo veritatis verius

There is nothing more true than this word of truth, in the terse Latin of the *Adoro te devote.* Or, in Gerard Manley Hopkins' translation of it beginning 'Godhead here in hiding':

Truth speaks truly or there is nothing true.

10

Grace

The doctrine of grace in the West largely derives from St Augustine, who as a result of his own life and conversion saw it especially as healing grace, in contrast with the emphasis of the Eastern Fathers on deifying grace which makes us like God. Healing grace heals fallen human nature, which has lost its freedom, by strengthening its weakness and giving the power to act well. Grace heals the will by making it free, so that it *loves* justice. St Thomas builds on Augustine but introduces two new elements: first, the idea of grace as a participation, which he took from Pseudo-Dionysius; and secondly, the Aristotelian idea of motion, that a movement of the will, as it is moved by grace, is involved in good actions. The questions on grace follows the section on the Old Law in St Thomas, since the law of the New Testament for him is the grace of the Holy Spirit. Since the love which fulfills the Law is poured into our hearts by the Holy Spirit, it makes us fulfill the commandments freely, that is willingly, by an inclination, or 'inner stirring (*instinctus*) of grace'.[1] St Thomas makes clear that grace derives from the Incarnation, since grace comes to us because Christ's humanity is 'full of grace'. Thus we are made sharers in the divine nature through his humanity.

By the very fact that the soul is made in the image of God it has an openness for divine life: *capax est dei per gratiam*, literally: it is capable of receiving God through grace.[2] We need grace to fulfill the potential which human nature has been made

[1] *Summa* I-II 106, 1.
[2] Augustine, *De Trintate* XIV c. 8.

with, since our destiny is not anything natural but lies beyond our natural power, just as an eye, however keen its power of sight, needs light to see things. Grace is God's means of leading us back to himself: 'by grace we are led back (literally, 'reduced') to God'.[3]

Grace springs from divine love and draws us above our natural state to share in divine goodness. It is the special love by which he draws the rational creature above nature to participate in the divine good. Grace is an effect of divine love impressed in us. God's love for us is called grace since he loves us as a free gift and not because of anything we do or deserve. Grace is the love by which we hold someone pleasing to us, so that they are loved by us. God loves all that he has made since all being is good in itself and he has given everything its natural existence, but it is only creatures capable of knowing and loving him, whom he loves with the love of friendship.[4] Charity itself is a certain kind of friendship which requires a reciprocal (mutual) loving, based on sharing something in common; in this case, it is sharing God's blessedness. There can be real friendship between God and man because we are made in the image of God and God loves us in his Son, who took our human nature to himself. Love involves communication between people, which is the basis of friendship. Thus some friendship is founded on the communication of God with man. That friendship arises when love is reciprocal does not imply that our love of God can ever equal God's love of us. Man enjoys friendship with God because God communicates with him, making us into his companions: 'God alone deifies us by communicating a partnership (*consortium*) in the divine nature by some shared likeness'.[5] Deifying, or divinizing, grace, as distinct from healing grace, is the characteristic idea of the Greek Fathers; at its simplest, it means union with God. 'We have been made sharers in divine life' (*2 Peter* 1, 4). Grace is a share in the divine nature since by it we participate in God's

---

[3] *Summa* I-II 111, 1.
[4] *Ibid.* I 20, 2 ad 3.
[5] *ibid.* I-II 112, 1.

own understanding and love of himself, which is the divine life. The rational creature is made a sharer in the divine Word and in Love proceeding, so that we are able to know and love God. But since this is not anything we can come to by our own power or virtue, it is as it is given us from above.

Grace is a participated likeness of the divine nature, as it makes us sharers in it. It is a *likeness* because it enables us to attain the likeness of God, in which we have been made; and it is a *participated* likeness because we share in divine nature by a likeness, by being recreated through grace.[6] Thomas' own idea of how we are made 'deiform' is that it is in the next life by the light of glory, when we have the vision of God, for which we need a special light, that is one which we do not have by nature, to strengthen our sight, for then 'we shall be like him when we see him as he really is' (*1 John* 3, 2). However, we shall see God immediately, face to face, not merely in some image or likeness of him.[7] As we shall be like God when we have the vision of him, and we need grace to have this vision, so we are made deiform by grace when we have the vision.

We need the help of grace to attain our final end, which is the enjoyment (*fruitio*) of God, since it surpasses nature: 'what the eye has not seen nor the ear heard nor the heart of man conceived' (*1 Corinthians* 2, 9). The vision of God exceeds that natural faculty of the intellect as the sun exceeds the power of the human eye. Thus we have to be raised up to something which is above our natural powers. Although the capacity to know God is natural, we need grace since the light we need to strengthen our sight for seeing God is not connatural to us. The desire is natural because we naturally desire to know the causes of things. But since the fulfilment of this desire, which cannot be in vain since it is put in us by nature, is supernatural because it lies in the vision of God, the fulfilment of it cannot be had without the help of a light, which is supernatural because it is not one we have by nature.[8] We are lifted up, literally 'sublimated', to the sight of God by a supernatural

[6] *Ibid.* I-II 110, 4.
[7] *Ibid.* I 12, 5.
[8] *Contra Gentiles* III c. 57.

light. In St Thomas light is twofold: there is the natural light of reason and the light of grace for what exceeds natural knowledge. We not only need grace for doing things but also for *knowing* certain things which are beyond the reach of unaided reason. Our beatitude consists in the vision of God, to which we are led by grace alone.

Grace is a disposition of soul as an habitual gift, which is sanctifying and healing grace; and it is divine assistance, which is active help and actual grace, for single choices and actions, moving us to do good. Sanctifying grace is given so that the soul is united with God, but we also need divine help for each action. Habitual grace may be compared with the state of a violin which has been tuned and is in tune, but merely being in tune does not of itself produce any notes unless someone actually plays the violin. The difference between habitual and actual grace is something like that between merely being in tune and producing some actual notes. In our fallen state we need grace to heal human nature, and for the supernatural virtues which join us with God. We also need grace since the Law does not enable us to rise from sin.

In Pelagius grace is the external help of the Law and the example of Christ. It is also the remission of sin. In his view, man can do enough to save himself by his own strength. In Luther we have the opposite: there is no natural good left in man. In St Thomas' view of human nature we have not been deprived of all natural good, since the natural powers of reason and will remain, but we are in a weakened state since their power is impaired. In Augustine's expression: the image in us has not been rubbed out altogether, for the outlines remain. We need grace but only some interior gift from God can dispose us to receive grace in the first place. However, we do not need some prior grace to dispose us for this grace and so on, since God is the First Mover.[9] When God moves the will, he draws, or attracts, us to himself. God brings it about that we choose him in the first instance but once we have chosen, or accepted, his grace by free choice, he continues his assistance

---

[9]*Summa* I-II 109, 6 and 3.

so that the good action or resolve can be carried right through. When this has been repeated many times, we are preserved in the good to the end. God works it that we want, but when we want he works with us that we bring to completion.[10] Operative grace is God's initiative, but without the response of free will it would work no further. There is a co-operation of God with man, though grace has the initiative, so that our actions are neither God's alone nor ours alone but are wholly God's and wholly ours. We are not merely passive in being helped by grace, as Luther would make us, but the active response of our will is also required, otherwise our actions are not truly voluntary, or meritorious. Grace does not supersede our natural powers but raises them to a higher level of action; it does not blot them out but perfects them.[11] St Thomas does not overlook nature but respects it and takes it into full account. Grace does not replace nature, since it is after all nature which grace is supposed to restore and raise up. Thus with St Thomas, we can neither do sufficient to save ourselves, as in Pelagius, nor are we incapable of any natural good but quite passive, as in Luther, but some natural good is left in us and it is neither God alone nor ourselves alone but there is a cooperation of God with man. St Thomas considers the case of whether someone is able to obey the natural law by their own strength, which he doubts is possible to do entirely consistently, but says that they will not do it for the highest motive, which is out of charity, that is for the love of God, without grace.[12]

For St Thomas grace is a reality, a *res*. This helps us see that theology is about *realities*. Grace does not just mean the way God looks on us or divine acceptance, as justification in Luther means that God does not count our sins against us, but it makes a *real* difference to us since it has positive effects, recreating and transforming us. St Thomas calls justification a change (*transmutatio*), by which we are ordered within to God.[13] Grace is not external or superficial but interior in its effects, since it

[10]Augustine, *De Gratia et Libero Arbitrio* 17.
[11]*Summa* I 1, 8 ad 2.
[12]*Ibid.* I-II 109, 4.
[13]*Ibid.* I-II 113, 2.

is not merely remission of sin but also works a change of the person for a new life by inner renewal. St Thomas already foresaw two of Luther's positions: that grace is merely divine acceptance of a person, and that it is not having our sins reckoned, or imputed, to us.[14] Luther makes justification a purely legal status of how we are looked on by God, without positive interior effects worked by him in us. For St Thomas grace is real, that is it is a reality, because it gives us a share in the divine life, which is something. In his presentation of grace St Thomas is but bringing out the significance of St Paul's phrase: 'the gift of grace is eternal life' (*Romans* 6, 23).

Grace puts something in the soul, as light puts something in the air it illumines. Light is something since it travels and its speed can be measured. Grace is like the light of the soul; it is the brightness (*nitor*) of the soul, which is obscured when sin casts a shadow across the mirror of the soul, so to speak, so that it loses some of its radiance and the clearness of its reflection.[15] Sin obscures the brightness of the soul since it is receding from the light of reason and divine law. The human soul, St Thomas says, has a twofold splendour, as it shines with the natural light of reason and with the divine light of grace. The beauty of the soul comes from its illumination by the divine light. One person has more grace than another by being more lit-up (literally, 'illustrated') by grace. We are lit up within by the presence of the godhead, as air is lit up by the presence of light.[16] Grace corresponds with the effects of sin: grace is light as sin darkens the soul; it strengthens the will by God drawing it to good, and sin weakens the soul; and it is remission of sin, as sin incurs guilt. Far from virtue being sufficient by itself to save us, we need grace since it is the root of virtue, which therefore presupposes it.[17]

Grace not only works like light but is a movement (*motus*), as thinking and willing are called movements of the mind by Aristotle, taking movement in a large sense.[18] Grace is a

[14]*Ibid.* I-II 110, 1.
[15]*Ibid.* I-II 110, 2.
[16]*Ibid.* I-II 112, 4.
[17]*Ibid.* I-II 110, 3 ad 3.
[18]*De Anima* III c. 4 429b25.

movement as everything requires divine power to lead it to an action beyond its natural power. Thus grace fits within St Thomas' view of God as the First Mover, who is the cause of all action. It is not just that one cause depends on another, but that all other causes depend on this one cause, the First Cause. All movement goes back to the First Mover. When God moves the will towards the good, he does not override the will but leaves it free, since he does nothing against our nature, of which he is the author, which is to act voluntarily. Only force or coercion is against freedom, but God does not move the will against its natural inclination, which is to the good. When God moves the will, he moves it freely because he moves it from *within*.[19] Only God can move the will from within, as he is in all things. In St Thomas' view of the world, there are primary and secondary causes. Secondary causes can retain their freedom, though they have a primary cause. The primary cause of everything is God, on whom everything depends for its power to move since it depends on him for its existence. But God gives things their own natural way of working, so that they properly cause things too. We might see an analogy for primary and secondary causes in government: the Prime Minister entrusts affairs to members of the Cabinet, who in turn may leave a certain amount to the judgment of their under-secretaries. Being caused is not contrary to freedom; it is determinism which takes away freedom. That we have the power to will anything at all comes from God, but that we will this or that lies within the power of choice given to us. We are not forced but *inclined* to the good by God. The will can be moved by another yet move voluntarily itself when this other is the cause of its voluntary nature. If the will were not inclined one way rather than another it might not choose at all; then it would not so much be free as inert. All this is quite different from Hume's view of moral action, for whom to be caused is to be necessitated, since he has no idea of a cause which leaves room for freedom, since he thought that we get the idea of cause from constant conjunction.[20] It is grace which enables us to be truly free to

---

[19] *Summa* I 105, 4 ad 1.
[20] *A Treatise of Human Nature* II iii 1.

choose the good which reason approves. God leaves the will free in moving it because it always retains the possibility of resisting grace. That free will is able to accept grace is a disposition caused by God but that grace, once offered, is accepted requires an act of will on man's part.

11

The Virtues

St Thomas begins his discussion of ethics, the virtues and their opposite sins, with the end of man, since that makes actions specifically human actions is that we do them with an intention for an end. Animals too act for ends but, unlike us, they do not know them as ends; they do not have reasons for what they do. The last end of man, St Thomas says, is beatitude since everyone naturally desires to be happy. Also happiness is our last end since we do not desire to be happy for some further end but happiness is something sought for its own sake. To reach our end we have to be disposed for it. The virtues are dispositions for acting well. As Aristotle said, we have been made to act well as the function of a harpist is to play the harp well.[1] Acting virtuously is not itself the blessed life, as Cicero maintained,[2] but virtue disposes us for it since only someone with right will is disposed to see God. Thus ethics in St Thomas is about the virtues, which dispose us for the vision of God. He builds on the ancient foundation of the four cardinal virtues: prudence, justice, courage and temperance, which perfect human nature, with the three theological virtues: faith, hope and charity, which join us to God. For St Thomas the final end of man is the *enjoyment* of God (*fruitio dei*). Thus his moral doctrine is not some stern teaching about duty or detachment but about our reaching the end for which we have been made, which is to enjoy something.

[1] *Nichomachean Ethics* Bk I c. vii.
[2] *Tusculan Disputations* Bk V.

The root of virtue is the desire for happiness, and happiness is the reward of virtue, Aristotle says.[3] Thomas argues that happiness lies in an activity since activity is the perfection of any existent thing. Ultimate happiness lies in the activity of the highest part of ourselves: the intellect. Since the perfection of the mind is knowing the truth, beatitude consists in contemplation of the truth.[4] The highest end is something done for its own sake and not for any further end; this is the consideration of the truth for its own sake and not for some practical end, as one might study physics to do astronomy. However, beatitude is not anything purely or merely intellectual in St Thomas' view since he also says that we are more drawn to God by love than by reason.[5]

There are two kinds of happiness: a natural one and one which lies beyond the attainment of our natural powers. To attain this further happiness we need virtue which is not merely natural but supernatural virtue. As Thomas says, we can only come to a more than natural happiness by some participation in the divine nature. This is given us by the supernatural virtues of faith, hope and charity. They are also known as the 'theological' virtues, since their object is not how we live with other men but is God; and as the 'divine' virtues, since not only is their object God but they are infused in us by God, since we cannot acquire them by our own natural powers.

Virtue is either acquired or infused. Acquired and infused virtue differ from one another not only in their source, as they either spring from human effort or from grace, but also in their end as one acts for a merely natural end or for an end beyond this world. The virtues are connected since they approach unity in us, whereas sin recedes from unity. The acquired virtues are united by prudence, which perfects reason, and the infused virtues by charity, which directs all the virtues to our last end, that is to God. The moral virtues of prudence, justice, fortitude and temperance, which subject the appetites to reason, are connected since a just man will often need courage

[3]*Ethics* I vii.
[4]*Summa* I-II 3, 5 ad 2.
[5]*Ibid.* I-II 26, 3 ad 4.

to uphold principle. We have courage and temperance since we can be deflected from our proper and noble ends and from the good of holding to reason either by fear of harm or by the attraction of pleasures. One cannot have the moral virtues without prudence, or prudence without the moral virtues since the virtuous man is most likely to judge rightly. Prudence is not just about being a good sailor or a good electrician or a good violinist, which is being good *at* things, but about the *whole* of one's life and living it well altogether. Prudence is about choosing the right means to the end in particular circumstances, discerning what to seek and what to avoid. Thus it is able to apply the moral principles one knows in a given situation. Prudence is the virtue for deliberating, or taking counsel, about what is to be done; it does not choose the end but the means to it. Prudence strikes a balance when one is faced with conflicting demands or alternatives, both of which are good in themselves, such as the claims of one's family and of others on oneself. It also does things for the right motive, neither out of rashness or on sudden impulse nor through partiality. We have a virtue of prudence since we are rational creatures, who deliberate and reason about what they are to do. So prudence perfects the reason for doing this activity well. Prudence is the highest of the moral virtues since the good of reason is the good of man. Prudence is governed by reason, charity by wisdom.[6]

Justice orders us to the common good of society, courage and temperance order a man in himself, and charity to divine good. Justice is rendering what is due or owed to another; charity is not an obligation or debt but is a spontaneous gift, though both justice and charity are an exchange.

The acquired virtues are human virtue, but for a more than natural or purely human end we need more than natural virtue to direct us to an end beyond nature. Faith, hope and charity are supernatural virtues since they raise our minds to things which are above nature. Faith is the first of these three because we have to apprehend something before it can be loved by the will. Charity is called the root of the virtues because it perfects

[6]*Ibid.* II-II 24, 1 ad 2.

faith and hope, though we cannot have charity without faith and hope because there cannot be friendship with someone we disbelieve or despair of.[7] Faith is prior because we cannot hope for beatitude unless we believe it is possible to attain, nor can we love anything we do not know. Charity loves God for his own sake. We cannot have beatitude without charity, which is the love of God; it would be like a man with no love of music being on a desert island with nothing to do but to listen to Bach. Only charity can *enjoy* God, which is what beatitude is.

Faith is an act of the intellect since it is *assent* to divine truth. As the proper object of the intellect is truth, the object of faith is the First Truth and other things, such as the Incarnation and sacraments, as they are our way to God. The object of faith is simple in itself, but since we only know simple things complexly in this life, we know it by means of propositions. However, the act of faith does not end in a proposition but in a reality; we only form propositions to have knowledge about realities, as we also do in science.[8] Faith leads to the vision of God because it contains the elements of what we will have sight of. Faith is 'the substance (*argumentum*) of things hoped for' (*Hebrews* 11, 1), since we hope to be made blessed by the vision of that which we adhere to by faith. It is a disposition of the mind by which eternal life is begun in us, since eternal life consists in the vision of the things we hold now with faith. Hope comes into this definition of faith because it is in things not yet seen. Since it is in things not seen, faith differs from science and intuition. It lacks the clearness of science since the matters of faith are above reason. Though faith lacks the clearness of science, which is about things we can see, it does however have greater certitude than science because of the greater authority on which it rests, which is not human understanding but the Word of God, who can neither deceive nor be deceived. As St Thomas says, the motive for belief is the authority of God's word and the inner inspiration of God inviting one to believe.[9] We assent to

[7] *Ibid.* I-II 65, 5 ad 2.
[8] *Ibid.* II-II 1, 2 ad 2.
[9] *Ibid.* II-II 2, 9 ad 3.

things not seen on divine authority. For faith two things are required, both of which come from God: things to be believed, which have been revealed by God and are proposed for belief; and a motive for believing them, which moves the will, since the mind also requires an interior motive as well as evidence from outside, for not all who saw the miracles which Jesus performed believed in him. Therefore something else besides the mere sight of the evidence moved those who did believe in him. Faith is also a supernatural gift because by it the mind is raised to things which are above what is known by natural reason alone.

Because it is not science, faith is *imperfect* knowledge, since it does not see the things it assents to. Nevertheless, even though it is imperfect knowledge, faith perfects the intellect since it raises the mind to things above nature and unites us with divine truth, for it is better to know a little about higher things than much about lower ones. As it is the 'argument' of things hoped for, faith differs from opinion since, though it does not apprehend the First Truth as it is in itself, it is firm *adhesion* to the truth which is not apparent to us now. Faith is nothing other than a participation in, or adherence to, the Truth.[10] Faith is obscure but has certainty. It is an 'imperfect' virtue by nature of the virtue itself, which does not see its object clearly, but not in the sense that one cannot have perfect or complete faith, for its virtue lies in the firmness with which one holds to the truth which is not yet seen. The perfection of faith does not come from the way its object is known but from its certitude and the firmness of its adhesion to its object.

Faith is 'enigmatic' knowledge. When St Paul said that we see now in a riddle (*en ainigmati*), he was probably thinking of *Numbers* 12, 8, when God told Aaron and Miriam that he would not speak to them face to face, as he did to Moses, but in 'enigmas and figures'. The imperfection of the virtue of faith may be partly removed by the gift of understanding, which St Thomas says makes us 'intuit the things of faith clearly and limpidly'.[11] We know the invisible things of God enigmatically

---

[10] *In II Timotheum* c. 2 lect. 2.
[11] *In Isaiam* c. XI.

(*sub aenigmate*) by faith, but to know them perspicaciously (*perspicue*) in a higher than merely human way belongs to the gift of understanding. Understanding brings insight into and penetrates to the heart (*ad intima*) of the things, which faith assents to and reason cannot fathom. The gift of understanding perfects the virtue of faith, which by itself is dark assent. It lights up (*illustrat*) the mind about things which surpass natural reason and which we come to by faith from hearing. It also disposes us for the vision of God since it purifies the mind of wrong images of and errors about God. Thus this gift goes with the Beatitude, 'Blessed are the pure of heart, for they shall see God'. The heart is also purified of its disordered affections by the gifts of fear, piety and fortitude.

The gifts are helps for the virtues, which dispose someone for following the prompting (*instinctus*) of God.[13] As animals are moved naturally by instinct, so we are moved by a spiritual instinct, or sense, to follow God. The gifts are perfections of the powers of the soul, rendering it movable by the Holy Spirit and making us responsive to divine inspirations. The gifts differ from the virtues since they do not choose but *direct*; also they do not increase, as the virtues do. Although some of the gifts have the same name as virtues, they differ from the virtues since the virtue of courage, for instance, does not inspire confidence in God, as the gift of courage does. The gift of fortitude is itself directed by the gift of counsel, which St Thomas observes we need because our deliberations are 'timid and unsure'. The Holy Spirit both instructs the mind and moves the heart, since he enlightens the mind with the gift of counsel about what is to be done and moves the heart.[14] Although the gifts perfect the virtues, they are not higher than the supernatural virtues since they presuppose them; faith and charity precede them since they unite us with God, whereas the gifts are for following God. To be movable by the Holy Spirit we first have to be subject to him, which we are by the gift of fear, which perfects the virtue of hope.

[12] *Summa* II-II 8, 1.
[13] *Ibid.* I-II 68, 2.
[14] *In Romanos* c. VIII lect. 3.

The object of hope is twofold: the future good which one desires and the help by which one expects to attain it. Thus God is the object of hope, which makes it a theological, or divine virtue, as we hope for eternal beatitude and it reaches up to him by relying on his help to attain beatitude. Hope makes us inhere in God as the source of perfect goodness, as we depend on his help for obtaining eternal good. Hope is both of future happiness and trust in present help to come to it. The contrary of hope, which is despair, does not have a true idea of God since it does not think that salvation and pardon can come from him.

Although hope and fear are contrary, the virtue of hope and the gift of fear go together since they both produce humility: hope, as we do not presume to rely on our own strength; the gift of fear, as it overcomes pride in inspiring the reverence by which we are subject to God. God is the object of fear as well as of hope, since fear takes away presumption, which is against hope since it takes God's mercy for granted and despises his justice, relying on oneself, whereas hope looks to God for help. Fear fears God's justice and hope hopes in his mercy. Hope looks to the good and fear flies from evil. There are two kinds of fear: servile and filial. Servile fear fears God out of fear of punishment; filial fear fears rather to offend or to be separated from him. It is only this second kind of fear which goes with charity and is a gift of the Holy Spirit. Filial fear is the beginning of wisdom: 'The fear of the Lord is the beginning of wisdom' (*Psalm* 111, 10). For with the gift of fear our life is directed by godly reasons and we are ruled by God in everything.

Wisdom is the gift of spiritual judgment: 'the spiritual person judges all things' (*1 Corinthians* 2, 15). Wisdom judges by the divine truth to which faith assents and which understanding penetrates. Wisdom does not judge by reason alone but with a certain 'connaturality' with what one is talking about, as a just man speaks about justice in another way than an unjust one. Thus St Thomas, quoting from Pseudo-Dionysius, says that the theology which is not just learning but also affects one's life goes with a gift of the Holy Spirit: 'not only learning but also undergoing what one studies', *non solum discens sed etiam patiens.*[15] Wisdom goes with experience. To judge about divine matters not merely in the light of natural reason is a gift of the Holy Spirit. Wisdom participates in a likeness of the Son who is begotten Wisdom.[16] We also have a gift for judging about created and human things, for, as St Thomas remarks, created things by themselves do not arouse spiritual joy, unless they are referred to the divine good. This seems to be true of the Romantic poets at the end of the eighteenth and in the early nineteenth century, in whom we find a spirit of melancholy and sadness pervading their deification of nature. The gift which relates the study of created things to God is that of knowledge.

The gift of wisdom is associated with charity, which St Thomas defines as a kind of friendship. For the background of this we have to turn to Aristotle on friendship, in Books VIII and IX of the *Nicomachean Ethics*. Not love but friendship is the virtue for Aristotle, since in his view love is rather an act of passion but friendship is a disposition and truly being friends includes having other virtues, when we love others for what they are, which means what is good and likable in them. There are three kinds of friendship: for what we can get from the other (what is useful); for the pleasure of sharing some common activity, such as sailing or botany; and for the sake of the other person. Only good people can be friends in this third and truest way, for bad people cannot love one another for their own sake. Aristotle describes some of the characteristics of friendship as follows: friends enjoy the same things together, share one another's joys and sorrows, delight in one another's company; 'nothing is so characteristic as friends spending time together'. Those are most truly friends, he says, who desire the good of their friends for *their* sake. In Aristotle, however, there is nothing about the virtue of charity; he goes no higher than human friendship. Charity in St Thomas is first and foremost friendship with God. God is to be loved first because he is the source of our happiness.[17] One of the effects of friendship is that the presence of the other person makes one happy.

[15]*Summa* I 1, 6 ad 3.
[16]*Ibid.* II-II 45, 8.
[17]*Ibid.* II-II 24, 2 ad 2.

Charity rather than love is friendship because love can be one-sided but it has to be reciprocal for it to be friendship. Also there has to be some affinity and likeness between friends. A man can have love (*amor*) for a horse but cannot be friends with a horse. Horse and rider for instance, do not share riding in the same way as two riders share riding together. What turns love into friendship is the desire for the other's good rather than one's own. Charity also adds society, companionship and mutual love to *amor*. Charity is not mere benevolence since it does not derive from human virtue but from God. Yet surely much love of charity is not mutual or reciprocated, as in giving alms or helping the poor? Is this then not charity because there is no mutual love? Although there may appear to be no friendship, the poor love their benefactors out of gratitude to them and in this way there is mutual love. Secondly, even if there is apparently no mutual love, helping the poor is still charity since the love of our neighbour is itself a participation in the divine charity.[18] For the love of God and the love of others are not two loves but it is by the same act of love that we love God and others because we love them in the light of God. What we desire for them with charity is the good which we hope for from God ourselves, and what we ought to desire for them is that they be in God.[19] But how can there be mutual love between God and man, seeing the great distance between ourselves and God? Friendship with God is possible since there is an affinity as we are in the image of God and God loves us in his beloved Son, who took our human nature to himself. Our love of others is founded on the image of God, which constitutes our likeness to them, and on our capacity to share the same beatitude, on which friendship with God is founded, as all friendship is based on sharing something. However, our love of God can never equal his love for us; the most we can do is to love God with the whole of ourselves, and in this way we can love God perfectly. God's love goes out to us; we return love to him and our love overflows to others in a circular movement of love.[20]

---

[18]*Ibid.* II-II 23, 2 ad 1.
[19]*ibid.* II-II 25, 1.
[20]*Ibid.* II-II 27, 4 ad 2.

Charity is the source of our good deeds since it directs all the other virtues to our last end. 'The end of all human actions and affections is the love of God, by which especially we reach our final end.'[21] Charity contains all the virtues since it fulfills the Law, which presupposes them for its keeping. Love is the end of the Law because the intention of divine law is primarily that someone adheres to God. The purpose of the commandments is a life of friendship with God since the end of the commandments is charity, which sums them up. The love of God and of our neighbour, St Thomas says, are contained in the Ten Commandments as principles are in conclusions drawn from them, for they all come under either of these two.[22] Since all the infused virtues are connected by charity, so that none of them can be had without it, one act which destroys charity loses them all, since charity depends wholly on its source, which is God. Thus one sin, when it is quite contrary to God, can lose all grace, just as an obstacle can shut out the light completely from its source and bring darkness.[23] As light disappears the moment an obstacle excludes it, so charity and grace can be extinguished when someone turns away from God, the source of charity, completely. If Aristotle could call justice the sum of the virtues since it enters all of them as they are about living in human society,[24] Aquinas might have said the same about charity, since no virtue is perfect without charity. Charity is an infused virtue since it transcends human power, being based on sharing something which is itself a gift to us. 'Since charity transcends human nature, it does not depend on natural virtue but solely on the grace of the Holy Spirit.'[25] Charity is also the transcendent virtue since it runs through all the infused virtues, which do not exist without it. Charity is an effect of the Holy Spirit dwelling in us. Since the rule of the Holy Spirit in us is inner liberty, charity which comes from the Holy Spirit makes us truly free.

---

[21] *Ibid.* II-II 27, 6.
[22] *Ibid.* I-II 99, 1 ad 2.
[23] *Ibid.* II-II 24, 12.
[24] *Ethics* V c. 1 1130a9.
[25] *Summa* Ii-II 24, 3.

Charity is not just doing good, as mere benevolence might be, but is primarily union with God. Union is not so much a result of charity as charity *is* union with God itself.[26] Charity is the only one of the theological virtues which unites us with their object immediately. If faith did this, it would no longer be faith, which is in things unseen, but clear vision. We no longer need hope when we have attained that which we hoped to reach. Charity is the sharing of a spiritual life, by which we come to beatitude.[27] Friendship with God is a familiar conversation but our conversation with God in this life is imperfect; it will only be perfect in our heavenly homeland when we reach our goal.[28]

[26] *Ibid*. II-II 24, 12 ad 5.
[27] *Ibid*. II-II 25, 2 ad 2.
[28] *Ibid*. II-II 23, 1 ad 1.

12

Prayer and Providence

We pray for things because they come within divine providence. Unless things fall within God's providence, he could not do anything about them and there would be no point in praying to him about things that lie outside his power. St Thomas says that two mistakes are made about prayer: (1) that we can alter the mind of God by prayer, and (2) that it is useless, that it has no effect at all, which is that it is not a cause of anything. Since both these misunderstandings about prayer spring from a false view of providence, we should consider providence before we discuss prayer. It is perhaps to be expected that providence will be overlooked in a scientific age, which thinks that everything can be explained by the laws of nature without needing the guidance of any other power. Since prayer is asking for things to be brought about by divine assistance, it is clear that it is no use praying if the world is not governed by divine providence, for there would be no use in praying to God if there are actions outside his control and about which he does not have knowledge since they do not come within his providence. Without divine providence there is no reason for hope in God, since things could turn out in a way which was beyond his power.

Providence means that we live in a universe in which things do not merely happen by chance, nor by blind necessity, but which is a rational universe. Pure chance and determinism are contrary to the idea of providence since either implies that the world is not ruled by anyone. Chance would mean that there is no order at all, determinism that everything is fixed inexorably. As we have seen, the world is not necessitated since it is not created out of necessity but freely and also because it comes from a mind, which includes will. Providence is God's idea of ordering everything to an end, which is the divine good. Its source is divine wisdom. Although it is certain and unfailing, it includes freedom since the execution of God's plan also includes secondary causes. Although there are primary and secondary causes, it would be mistaken to think that events are partly due to God and partly due to created causes; rather, they are brought about *wholly* by God and *wholly* by secondary causes because natural things produce their own effects in virtue of God (*in virtue divina*) since nothing can act apart from his power, for they depend on him for keeping them in existence.[1] They only have any power to act because they depend on him for their existence.

Thus providence extends as far as God's causality does, which is to all things, since God is the cause of all existence and he keeps all things in existence. If anything were excluded from his providence, it would be annihilated since it would escape the universal cause of existence, on which everything depends for its existence. As everything depends on the First Cause, so nothing happens outside the order of providence: 'Not one sparrow falls to the ground without God knowing about it'.[2] There is not any getting outside divine providence since, though a potter is outside the pot he makes, God is not outside his creation but in it, sustaining it in existence.

The universe has the coherence it does, which is manifest in its order, because it is ordered to an end. God does not just bring things into existence but orders them to an end, the good. There is nothing existent which does not participate in some way in divine good since God is the cause of all existence and the being of things is good in itself.[3]

Nonetheless, though mere chance or necessity is contrary to providence, providence includes chance and necessity. Something happens by chance when it is unintentional. There can be chance and necessity within providence when chance and necessary things are led back to some higher cause, which

[1] *Contra Gentiles* III c. 70.
[2] *Matthew* 10, 29.
[3] *Summa* I 23, 4 ad 1.

they can be because even when things occur by chance through some cause failing or being prevented by another cause, this cause depends on the First Cause for its existence. There clearly is some determinism in nature since it is possible to predict eclipses. It is interesting that St Thomas can find a place for fate.[4] Fate means that everything is subject to the necessary motion of the stars and planets. However, not everything can be due to fate since human actions are not directly subject to the heavenly bodies but to will, which does not necessarily follow the inclination of nature. St Thomas' method of showing that not everything comes under fate is first to ask what kind of action the heavenly bodies have. They have one effect since they are natural agents; so they cannot be the cause of accidental and chance things, which arise from a cause being impeded by another one. Thus at least some things go back to another cause than fate. The error about fate comes in regarding it as the primary cause when it belongs to secondary causes. There is fate in the sense that predetermined intermediary causes come within providence but not in the sense of ruling everything, for the overall ordering of everything belongs to divine providence. Necessity comes within providence since God is the author of nature and natural things are not aimless but directed to their ends.

Providence also includes contingency since secondary causes can fail either through defects or free will. Free wills can fail, that is be defective in their choice, because God does not impede the will in its choice. Providence does not impose necessity on everything but it is certain because everything happens in the way which God foresees; but he wills this to be necessarily for some and contingently for other things. Something is contingent if it might or might not happen or exist, that is, it is not predetermined in its cause. Far from chance being contrary to providence it presupposes it since we would not talk about anything being unintended unless something were intended. Thus chance proves rather than disproves providence. Chance defects presuppose providence since things

---

[4]*Ibid.* I 116, 4.

only escape from causes because they are preserved by other causes which depend on the First Cause themselves.

If everything comes within divine providence, one might wonder how evil exists, since this too must be something under divine control. Evil comes within providence because free will does. If the will is properly free, there is the possibility within providence that it will sometimes choose wrongly. Evil itself is not intended by providence but it falls within providence because even evil can lead to good, as the evil done by persecutors is a cause of the virtue and reward of martyrs.

It is because not everything is necessary but some things are contingent that it makes sense to pray for them. However, prayers are not effective because they alter God's plan of providence but because they are part of it.[5] Prayer does not change providence, which is certain, but providence includes prayer as one of the causes of things, as it is due to divine ordering that some things are to come about by recourse being had to prayer. We do not obtain things because of the prayer for them but because God grants some things which he knows will be asked for in prayer. If prayer does not influence or change God's mind, which is immutable, what use is there in praying, since it would seem not to make any real difference whether we pray or not? When we pray we do not make known our needs and desires to God, who knows them already since he knows all things, but we pray to show that we truly want and long for what we ask for, and to *dispose* ourselves to receive what God in his providence has arranged as an answer to prayer. Prayer also arouses in us humility since it makes us realize our need for divine help. Thus it rouses trust in God. In this way prayer involves hope, which looks to God for help. Prayer also presupposes faith which believes it is possible to obtain things from God and that he is the source of all good.

Even when prayer does not obtain what it asks for but remains unanswered, it is still of value, that is it is worth doing, since it increases charity in us as it expresses our desire. What we should chiefly ask for in prayer is that we be united with

[5] *Contra Gentiles* III c. 96.

God, which is charity.[6] God himself inspires in us the desires we express in prayer. We do not move God by prayer; rather, he moves us to pray. We approach prayer from a prompting of the Holy Spirit, St Thomas says. Although we do not always know what it is good to ask for, the Holy Spirit inspires us to ask for the right desires. When the Holy Spirit is said to intercede for us, this means that he makes us pray for things which are for our good in accord with the will of God.[7] Both what we obtain through prayer and the prayer itself are God's gift, since it is not due to our prayer but to divine grace that prayer is answered and it is his grace which draws us to pray in the first place. The things for which we are to pray especially, says St Thomas, are those things which will lead us to beatitude. Since prayer springs from the desire of charity we pray always when this desire is continually in us either actually or virtually. The desire of charity makes prayer continuous. In this St Thomas interprets our Lord's command to pray without ceasing,[8] so that prayer can be assiduous although we have to be occupied with many other daily tasks. It is this desire, from which prayer comes forth, which ought always to be in us.

When we pray we give over (*tradit*) our minds to God. Prayer, in the definition of St John Damescene which St Thomas gives, is a rising of the mind to God (*oratio est ascensus mentis in deum*). Prayer is an act of the mind since it is by the mind that we apprehend what we ask for. But it is in act of the mind moved by the will, so it also comes from the heart, since we are moved to prayer by charity. We do not always need to use words in prayer, but words may help to stir up inner devotion by which the mind rises to God. As things we see can lead us to know about invisible things, so devotion is stirred up by consideration of the things which arouse the love of God, the chief of which, St Thomas says, is the humanity of Christ.[9] On how long at a time we should spend in prayer, he advises that it should last as long as it is useful for arousing the fervour of desire.

[6] *Summa* II-II 83, 1 ad 2.
[7] *In Romanos* c. VIII lect. 5.
[8] *Luke* 18, 1.
[9] *Summa* II-II 82, 3 ad 2.

However, St Thomas knew well that through out infirmity the mind cannot remain on the heights of prayer for long and that it wanders. Even when this happens, prayer does not lose its benefits since it is sustained by the *intention* with which it is directed to God from the outset, which lasts throughout the prayer, just as an arrow continues of itself on the course of its flight with the aim it was given at the start.[10] But for prayer to bring us consolation and to refresh us, we also need to have *attention* besides intention in prayer. Attention does not necessarily mean that one attends to every word one says but that one attends to the end or object to which prayer is directed, which is to God.

St Thomas might seem to have little to say under prayer about what many would understand by and look for under 'prayer', that is silent prayer, since for him prayer seems rather to be asking for things. For what we call prayer today we have to turn to another section of his writing, where he treats contemplation. Prayer, however, is connected with contemplation, since it is by prayer that we ask for the gift of wisdom, which lies in considering the truth. St Thomas defines contemplation simply as the consideration of the truth. The contemplation of divine truth is the goal of human life, since knowing divine truth is the final perfection of the mind. Contemplation is the end of human life even on this earth, since it is the beginning of beatitude, which is the end we are made for, and it leads us to it. But we only have it *imperfectly* in this life.

The end of contemplation is seeing the truth, which is an act of the intellect. But contemplation is not purely intellectual in St Thomas, as it may seem to be, since the truth for him is not only something to be apprehended but also to be *loved*: 'this is the ultimate perfection of the contemplative life, that the divine truth is not only seen but also loved'.[11] Contemplation in itself is done by the mind but it has its source in the affection, since someone is stirred to the contemplation of God by

---

[10] *Ibid.* II-II 83, 13 ad 2.
[11] *Ibid.* II-II 180, 7 ad 1.

charity. St Thomas would have seen the consideration of all truth, as it is studied by various branches of science, as having a part in contemplation as it can lead to knowledge of God. How then does the contemplation of the truth, which is also prayer, differ from any consideration of the truth, as someone may do this in a purely philosophical way? They differ by the charity with which the first is done. We only come to a simple view of the truth, he says, by degrees. Contemplation itself differs from prayer in two respects: prayer is asking *for* things, whereas contemplation is not done for any further end but for its own sake. And, secondly, greater charity and delight accompany contemplation, for someone might pray for something they wanted without much charity or much liking of prayer but more for what they wanted.

It is charity which perfects us. It will only be perfect in our heavenly homeland. Then faith will give way to vision and charity alone enjoy God in seeing the truth which makes us blessed. It was characteristic of the prayer of St Thomas to long for the sight of that to which we hold on to by faith now and can only talk about in this life with our inadequate words.

Index